DANCE FOR LIFE

JULIA FRANKS

Copyright © 2024 by Julia Franks

All rights reserved.

No part of this book may be reproduced in any form or by any electronic or mechanical means, including information storage and retrieval systems, without written permission from the author, except for the use of brief quotations in a book review.

Artwork by Finola Kinloch.

Contents

Preface	v
Introduction	vii
1. My Journey	1
2. The Origins of Dance and Human Evolution	22
3. The Rediscovery of Dance	40
4. The Place of Dance in today's world	62
5. Conscious Dance practices today	82
Acknowledgments	103
Bibliography	105
End Notes	107

Preface

The first time I met Julia Franks, she invited me to dance! Not personally, but via a mailshot in May 1988, just as the 'Second Summer of Love' was revving up in London. Julia wrote to me about a party night she was organ-
ising where young Londoners and young visitors to London could dance together, away from the West End Clubs and their predictable sounds, patterns, and prices. The invitation was too good to ignore, and I bought 50 tickets for my international students who craved the chance to mix and match with London locals on the dance floor.

Over the next 5 years I attended almost every event that Julia and her group ran, from massive raves in old industrial estates, to boat parties on the River Thames, Jam sessions in remote locations, and 'signature nights' at well-known London venues. People flocked to the dance floor: a compelling experience of pure joy and collective energy. Julia transitioned into practicing psychotherapy after the rave scene, and the first event she ran was for inspired clubbers who wanted the magic of dance but without the comedown of chemicals. She called it 'Spirit in the House'. This neatly captures her core idea; that music and dance are inspiring activities that can deepen human experience.

For the past 10 years Julia has been training in, and leading, conscious dance sessions. I've attended many of them. As Julia explains, conscious dance is not the opposite of unconscious dance, but rather of self-conscious dance. It's dancing without the self-consciousness that constrains us, and makes us shy, rigid, or stuck. This suddenly all makes sense. What she is about is reclaiming everyone's ability to dance as if no one is watching, even on a crowded dance floor. This call to uninhibited dancing is the key focus of her practice, to unlock human energy from stale patterns, narrow movement, or from constraining thoughts and misgivings. It is the reclaiming of a birthright, as she so clearly explains.

Dance for Life has a clarity and intuitive logic to it, that is like a dance itself. The 5 chapters each have their own rhythm, beat, and lyric. There is pace, flow, and shape. We learn how she encountered dance and placed it at the centre of her life. Julia recounts the story of how dance enabled human evolution and civilisation, but also how we 'lost' dance. She observes how the last 50 years have fostered the rediscovery of dance world-wide. She illustrates and demonstrates how dance is a force for good in our vulnerable world. Finally, we are introduced to what conscious dance is, and its many varieties. Along the way, we meet historians, anthropologists, psychologists, religious teachers and (most important) lots of wonderful ordinary people who dance with Julia every week, as I do.

Julia is uniquely qualified. As a former club promoter, current therapist, and conscious dance leader, Julia has curated 'dance experiences with a purpose' for more than 30 years and has danced with more than 1,000,000 people. Julia has been convening people and curating dance all her life, she wants everyone to get dancing. This book is a celebration of how dance can make us whole.

Prof Greg Clark CBE, Fellow, Academy of Social Sciences

Introduction

This book is an invitation. An invitation to start dancing again. An invitation to reclaim your love of life though the magic of dance. There is something about dancing that is restorative and enabling of the human spirit. It is at once physical, social, and emotional: a tribal form of collective expression. In my mind, there are 4 different kinds of people who might be interested in this book:

- People like me, dancers, exploring a deeper meaning to life: and how dance can enrich us.
- People interested in wellbeing who want to understand the role of the moving body and to unlock its treasures.
- People looking for a practice to do today which involves dancing with others for community and connection.
- People who are just interested. Curiosity may have drawn you here. You are very welcome too!

A Call To Dance

You may think you can't dance. It doesn't matter. *As the Zimbabwean proverb says:*

> *'if you can walk you can dance', and even if you can't walk, you can still dance.*

> *Here's what to do: choose a piece of your favourite, uplifting music. Take a couple of deep, slow breaths. Set a timer for 5 minutes. Play your music and follow your body as it moves to*

Introduction

the music. Any sort of movement, big beats or small is fine. After 5 minutes, check in with yourself: ask 'how am I feeling?'. Chances are more upbeat than you were 5 minutes before!

As I shall explain, I'm an adult woman in her 50s, who, every year, dances for hundreds of hours, and leads dance sessions for people of all ages and backgrounds. Dancing is a human birth right (as chapter 1 reveals), something our ancestors practiced and took for granted until our social norms changed, and our rules made it more difficult to dance freely. Now many of us are reclaiming that freedom to dance and are making space for this magic in our lives.

As we go along, I will share my story. I grew up in North London in the 70s, and 80s when multiple music cultures competed for the attention of young people, from soul, funk, and disco, to reggae, dub and ska, to the emergence of the house scene and the music genres it spawned in garage, drum n bass, trance, acid house & acid jazz, and the parallel growth of hip hop, rap, grime, and jungle. Along the way, these years carried pop, rock, punk, and the continuous returns to jazz, 'world music', Latin, and Afro beats.

In my teens and early 20s I was mesmerised by the richness of these music scenes and the dancing they inspired. With friends, we would dance for long deep hours. I became a promoter of club nights in London. My main work over a 10 year period was running raves, boat parties, improv and live jam sessions, and large scale dance nights for many thousands of people. In chapter 2 I recount how this evolved. The profound collective joy and transformation experienced by numerous people dancing together led me to a serious enquiry: how and why is dancing good for us?

I transitioned from promoting rave nights to becoming a psychotherapist and facilitator. I started my own workshop, 'Spirit in the House', for people who had been raving and wanted to find the meaning and purpose it might serve. We explored the ecstatic experience without taking drugs or drinking alcohol. We investigated the ecstasy of collective joy and sought ways to have it without chemicals. I married and started a family, and then built a psychotherapy practice. About 10 years later I started dancing again regularly. Not at night clubs and raves, but at conscious dance sessions that have grown rapidly in the past 20 years.

Chapter 3 covers the important context in the recent rediscovery of dance. The emergence of the New Age, or counter cultures, since the 1970 creates an important context in which dance is now being re-understood. The growth of meditation, yoga, other spiritual practices as well as emerging and revolutionary understanding of how our brains work have reached a startling and profound discovery: Our BODIES are intelligent eco-systems that store and hold our appetites, dreams, and aspirations, and also our traumas, sadness, yearnings, and memories. Through embodied practices we can establish a more intelligent and reciprocal relationship between body and mind, building a new alliance that serves our human needs. I've studied many forms of body work from Process Work to Open Floor Movement, and I will explain these in chapter 3.

One central form of this body work is dance. Since the 1970s we have reclaimed dance from the formulaic world of learned steps and styles, though of course they retain great value, and embraced the idea of free dance, with no set steps or patterns, and no right or wrong way to move. This shift from rule-based dancing to expressive dance mirrors many other changes in our society that also create the context in which dance is being re-evaluated. Dance is no longer seen primarily, or solely, as a form of entertainment, performance, celebration, match-making, or flirtation. It is now recognised as a health and wellbeing practice that serves both medical science, health needs and enhanced consciousness. Most profoundly, dance is a form of adults at play.

In this book, I will be talking about conscious dance. You could also call it dancing with awareness. Unlike many other forms of dance, there are no steps to learn. Conscious dance is about free expression, being invited to follow your own body's own impulses and patterns of

Introduction

movement, within a structured and led process. It is about freedom of movement. In a conscious dance practice you are offered a container, a space for your own unique dance to safely, and joyfully, evolve. I am not alone in having found this to be life-altering.

So how is dancing good for us? We'll look at this in some detail in chapters 3, 4, and 5. But let's start with a simple formulation.

- First, dancing is a form of physical exercise that can be as demanding as a gym session, a long run or ride, or a game of any sport. It is not only aerobically exercising, it also involves stretching, moving, and extending our bodies in ways that can increase our agility. We can extend our movement vocabulary in the ways that we can grow our vocabulary of words when we learn a language. Our bodies can become more supple, flexible, and expressive through dance, just as our heart and lungs get vigorously activated.
- Second, dancing is a social and collaborative activity. It is a team game. We dance with others, and they react and respond to us, as we do to them. We create the dance together and produce an experience that is both personal and social. This act of collaboration gives us each a sense of participation and belonging. We feel recognised and included, and we note how our own contribution has contributed to the dance. We feel our social agency.
- Third, dancing has a spiritual dimension. Like singing in a choir, the sharing of rhythms, rhymes, shapes, and patterns unites us in a sense of awe and wonder and allows our hearts to sore and our minds to quieten, as we open up to the spontaneous dance that can evolve from moving together in time. Studies have shown that people who dance regularly have enhanced empathic abilities.

Our dance sessions include meditation moments and 'inner dance' activities when we integrate the physicality of the dance with the spiri-

Introduction

tuality of breathing, still body, and quiet. So, a conscious dance session may feel more like a yoga class in some moments, a meditation session in others, and like a party, nightclub or gym session as well. It will often feel like all of these rolled into one.

With dance proven to provide these physical, social, and spiritual benefits, it is no surprise that much attention is now being paid to how dance can help us with health and social challenges from Isolation, and Depression, to Parkinson's, Dementia, Addiction, Obesity, and Stress. I will review how dance can increase health and wellbeing in chapter 4.

In chapter 5 I explain what the conscious dance scene is and describe how the different practices have evolved. From 5Rhythmstm, to Ecstatic Dance, to Open Floor, Movement Medicinetm, Biodanza, and Dance Movement Therapy, I review what each offers. I'll also introduce my own fusion practice called 'Flomotion'. It combines the core elements of conscious dance with my own music selections from the many years I've been dancing (there is a lot of funk, soul, and reggae at Flomotion sessions!).

As you'll see in the pages that follow, embracing conscious dance is about creating a different role for dance in our lives. It is *not* to place it in the small box of something only done at parties, weddings, bar/bat mitzvas, or at festivals, only when drunk, or only late at night, and in darkened rooms. Conscious dance is done at all times of day, when sober, usually in a gym, church hall, or public venue, and does not involve talking, pick up, or chat. Conscious dance is like going to a yoga session, where dance is the pathway into wellbeing.

I was not surprised to find that during the recent COVID-19 pandemic many people wanted to find ways to decompress without breaking the social distancing rules. During those hard months, my conscious dance practice, Flomotion, went online. Many people from all over the world gathered virtually on a weekly basis to dance together, enjoying the expression of freedom and connection that dance could bring into our own homes, despite the many restrictions we all faced. We even had a bring your parent night where there were 3 or 4 octogenarians present!

Introduction

COVID reminded us of the need for physical exercise, social collaboration, and shared emotional experiences. Dance, and especially online dancing, made these possible despite the obvious constraints.

Throughout the book you will find quotes from dancers who have shared the dance floor with me at Flomotion over the years. They have played an essential part in the evolution of Flomotion as a dance practice and have formed a supportive community. There would be no book without these people showing up (either in person or online) to make the dance happen, and I am immensely grateful to them.

There are also some personal reflections in the book. A sharing of my subjective experience, both of my history and in leading a dance practice. These elements: the voices of the Flomotion dancers and my subjective world, form a dance alongside the more prosaic parts of the book, providing different texture and shape to the reading experience. My hope is that they will awaken your curiosity and sound a call to the rhythm of your own dancing body.

As I said, the purpose of this book is an invitation. I want to invite you to consider putting dance back into your life. Whatever age you are, whatever shape and ability your body is in, and whatever background you have, I want to assure you that dance is genuinely for everyone, and it is not restricted to the young, fit, healthy, wealthy, or agile. It is for all of us, and the more of us who decide that dancing is rightly part of being human, the greater the options for dancing together there will be. It is especially important to reclaim dance as we get older. Our society has spread the profound untruth that dancing is mainly for the young and single. So, please consider my invitation and dance for life, on your own and with others when you can. I hope this book will help you accept the invitation.

ONE

My Journey

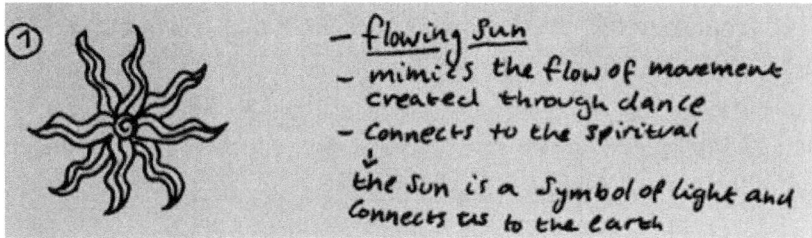

My beginning

It all starts with a love of dance... everything else is an afterthought.

For a long time - possibly from the very beginning - I knew intuitively that I loved to dance. For a long time I knew that I cared deeply about people and became interested in how we make change in our lives for the better. Only recently have I deeply understood the connection.

I used to think dancing was just about having fun. I still think it is. I have also discovered it's about many other things including a portal into feelings, connection, creativity and self-discovery.

This book is a point on a map. I am reaching out to you with experience, ideas and insights garnered over many decades from many different people. I hope it stimulates curiosity in you, taps into the wisdom in your own body, and that one day we might meet on the dancefloor.

> *Friday morning. The house hums with summer warmth, the laptop tip taps, the meeting of fingers, hands and mind. My body stills as I plumb its depth. Breath is my anchor.*

Let me create some context…

Dancing in North London

I grew up, the second generation in a Jewish family in North London. My grandparents were immigrants, fleeing persecution in Central/Eastern Europe. Their first language was Yiddish. They came from lives of survival steeped in the very old story of Jewish persecution, and the need to move on when they were either banished or driven out of the places they had called home.

My grandparents never wanted to talk about their past because it was too disturbing. They carried trauma. Freud's 'treatment' for mental disorders was in its infancy and it is only recently that we have come to understand that trauma is held in the body and needs careful containing attention in order to heal.

My parents came into a world of opportunity: post-war expansion, the aspiration of education and improving on the lives of their parents. I see now that theirs was an era of mind, and assimilation. Learn, read, understand, fit in. These were the tools to improve and flourish.

My father became a civil engineer initially with the intention of making his contribution to the new state of Israel. My mother, ever an anarchic spirit interested in new thinking, was a writer of fresh and challenging ideas. Myself, and my siblings, were always expected to go to University even though in that era only a minority of young people had this opportunity.

It wasn't that what happened in our bodies was nowhere to be found. There were parties, family gatherings, dancing, and joy. What hadn't happened yet was the discovery of the wisdom in the body.

> *I pause. My breath takes me deeper into memory: I am playing in my 'den' in the garden. An old bay tree that has a hollowed-out space in the middle, big enough for my child-shaped body. I sit for hours making 'mud pies' and immersing myself in sensory imaginal and sensory experience. I hear my mother telling people about this all those decades ago. I am embarrassed.*

Musical streams and waves

Wooshing forward in time, childhood years: a short spell of ballet, the informal dance performances for parents and friends, tapdancing, dance routines learned from the TV. It's the 1970s, London is quite a shabby place. Our parents took us to Sunday morning Jazz in an old boozer in King's Cross, New Merlin's Cave. I loved the music! I could feel that this was something exciting, rhythmic. And later family trips to Ronnie Scott's, where one night Ronnie himself told our chattering family table to 'shut up' and listen to the music. We also went to the Notting Hill Carnival on Family Day to look at the floats. Again, the sense of excitement at the heady mixture of music, rhythm, and dancing.

These musical experiences made deep impressions on my soul. I was receptive, hungry for more. I knew in my bones that these sounds and vibrations were my natural home.

> *Diary of a conscious dance teacher*
>
> *To present this process - a week in the life of a conscious*

movement teacher - I'm thinking sourdough bread making. Not that I've ever made any but hear me out.

Day one you put the ingredients together, mixing things up until you find the right consistency (the first attempt, the outline of a playlist). Thereafter for the next 6 days you have to 'feed the starter', adding and subtracting ingredients (tracks) as you go. Day 7: Bread-wise, you begin to see bubbles, and the yeast smell emerges (the joy of seeing the playlist come together). Finally, the bread is in the oven; it may take time to rise. (Finally the playlist is in the dance spac; we may take a time to warm up, but the ingredients are all there for a rich, embodied experience).

Diary of a conscious dance teacher, Sunday

Last night a group of us danced together in North London. I'm tired after the excitement of the evening. I wake up to some beautiful messages on the 'Flomotion Family' WhatsApp Group, people talking about being nurtured 'deep within' and the revitalizing nature of the community. I am so grateful to be part of this.

With the rhythms and energy of last night still fresh in my orbit, I am going to start next week's playlist. Having made hundreds of playlists for Flomotion, it has become much easier over time. I know the structure so well and the moods I want to create. In theory this should be a low-effort, undemanding Sunday pursuit.

Sometimes, for no obvious reason, I lose my compass. Despite my extensive playlists sorted into categories for each part of the dance, I can't quite decide where to start, what *to include. Nothing quite hits the spot. I am out of sorts, probably a bit outside my body. Other times it just flows like a stream just running its course, effortless, seamless, easy.*

I do some website admin, put together a mailout for this week's dance. Again, sometimes the graphic and the words come easy. Sometimes not. My compass changes and now I want to rest, come away from the big community connection and experience. I want to be quietly inside myself: reading, resting, walking, meditating, being with my husband.

School days and ways

My secondary education took place in a very mixed and multicultural comprehensive school in Inner London.

A sensory memory: our school is divided into 'houses'. One house was allowed to play music on a sound system sometimes at lunchtime. They played soul and reggae. It was a magnet for me; I wanted to be there, I wanted to be part of it, I wanted to dance!

Another clear memory: a young teenager, I am with a group at someone's house, and they are playing Ian Dury and the Blockheads. I am conscious that the lyrics are 'rude' and unlike anything I have heard before. I am aware that me and my friends are behaving in ways that are edgy and outside the bounds of school and family life.

The Punk Rock era: going down the Kings Road, Kensington Market, followed by the Mod era. We formed an all-female band at school, The Soft Centres. I was on guitar, backing vocals and I wrote songs. We did a gig at our school and one in my back garden at home. The boys' band always seemed to be the main act, the girls the warm up act.

People had record players in those days, often a box with a turntable on top. We would play vinyl LPs and later 12 inch singles. There were lots of parties, and after people had had enough to drink they might shift their awkward teenage bodies around to the music. Later, musicians would gather with electric guitars and drumkits to 'jam'.

Roots Train

I missed the big social scene in London whilst away at University. The studying side didn't engage me much either. What did interest me in my time at Sussex University was the University radio station. I ran a Sunday evening reggae show, with a London friend, called Roots Train. We took our home-made cassettes to the University studio, feeling smug and satisfied that we had 'cool' London music to offer others, most of whom were stuck on Echo and the Bunnymen and The Smiths.

After University, the only thing that I was interested in was counselling and psychotherapy. It had become increasingly clear that people wanted to confide in me, and that I was able to listen. However, no training course was willing to take on such a young person, so that interest had to wait until later in my 20s.

> *My heart. My heart is tender. I want to breeze through this part of the story but counsel myself to pause. Breath. Slow down. It's the story of me as 'the One Who Listens'. Many years of subsequent therapy adding new narrative, new layers. Like lines of sedimentary rock in fossils. There is a big back story here concerning attention and childhood adaptation. It is an ongoing story with a long timeline embedded in my soul.*

West Africa

A memory: my sister went to teach in Sierra Leone, West Africa, with Voluntary Services Overseas.. I decided to visit her for a few weeks.

Dance for Life

Life there in a very remote village was basic: no electricity or running water, a latrine in the back yard. We drank palm wine, Poyo, in the dark of the evenings. There were lots of opportunities to dance, including at a wedding where I couldn't believe that we danced and danced for hours on end. This was new. Feet shuffling, conserving the body's energy to keep moving, on and on.

One night, there was a special event. A temporary space created under the hot African sky; the perimeter fencing erected from palm trees. Generators were brought in to power the sound system and to cool the beers. My memory, going back more than 30 years lives in my body. I danced the whole night, hours and hour of moving and swaying to the beat. Sweat, smell, inclusion. A riotous joy under the stars, the rhythms and sounds seeping deep in my bones.

London Seen

It's the 1980s. Two of my amazing London friends, Nick Turner and Rob Sable had started to run live music nights in the back rooms of pubs. I got involved as a 'club promoter' mainly because I loved the vibe, I loved dancing. Together we set up 'London Seen' an entertainment night for foreign students visiting London, where there was music and a young local crowd to meet. There were nights with Latin bands and boat parties with our own sound system/DJ going up and down the Thames.

The house music scene was emerging at this time, and we started to run nights with well-known DJs and jam sessions with professional musicians. It was exciting, fun and I got to dance... a lot!

Superstition

The biggest event was a Saturday night down in Russell Square called Superstition. We hired a big student union space. The walls were decked with black sheeting and groovy banners made for a club; ultra-violent lights creating funky shapes all around the room. In the main room, a well-known house DJ, CJ Mackintosh had a residency. In the side room, musicians would gather for live jam (improvised) music. There was a tremendous atmosphere: uplifting, exciting, people connected and friendly. The night always ended with Stevie Wonder's track Superstition.

There was generally a long queue outside; I was often on the door at the beginning of the evening. Friends were paid to take money and check the guestlist, as well as run the cloakroom. Everything was cash in those days. I would collect a load of cash from the door. One of the bouncers would accompany me to a back room in the building where I would count and store all the notes. This would happen several times throughout the evening.

Other nights that we ran were: Turnmills in Clerkenwell, Dingwalls and HQs in Camden, Woody's in Westbourne Grove, the Starlight Club in Paddington.

> *A fleeting reflective moment, felt somewhere in the back of my body. I 'see' myself: this young woman immersed in a world that is no longer mine. Sadness. The unreachable past.*

> I danced a lot as a teenager in the 70s, at Discos. The Barry White era! The early 80s shifted me into Soul, Funk, and World Music, and then I started more serious dancing in the late 80s with Julia and her team that ran Superstition and other club nights in London. This was not just dancing, it was tribal. It awoke something deep in me. A sense of profound connection on the dance floor. Connection with others and with self.
>
> When Julia started Flomotion about 30 years after the first Superstition, I had to be there. And there it was again! This sense of profound and free connection with others and self, fused through the movement of bodies in

time, fuelled by amazing music direct from the human soul.

By breathing deep, the music literally dances us, if we are willing to let it do so. This letting go…… of shyness, fear, stress, distraction, or tiredness, allows energy in, and recharges the spirit.

Goyo Houlihan

Raves

By 1988 warehouse parties and raves were springing up all over the place. We used to go out in the car round the M25 looking for these events, often to the East or outskirts of London. My body remembers the euphoric feelings of staying up all night, hours and hours of dancing, meeting every sort of person, watching the sun come up. There were always those who had partied too hard, 'casualties', adrift in the early hours. Still living the dream, the hope, not wanting the party to end.

Acid Jazz and Acid House

Looking back, the move towards the acid house scene was a big deal. It crossed both cultural and class boundaries in a way the nightclub scene hadn't. To use Emma Warren's term: it *'democratised the dancefloor'* offering people the opportunity to dance any way they wanted, without having to look or move in any particular way.

I remember going to a big rave in East London. We met a load of people from Thamesmead. Working class and speaking with very different accents from the crowd from the Wag Club and those I was used to mixing with. I felt self-consciously posh and middle class around them. Dancing united us; it was a great leveller. We all loved the vibe and that was more important than our differences.

Amy Jenkins, writer of TV series This Life, expressed the scene well:

> 'We were moving on from the elitism of the 80s: the New Romantics, the dominance of the City, shoulder pads and Thatcher. We ditched dressing up and went to nightclubs in jeans and trainers instead. The E made us friendly - we didn't turn up coke-filled noses at each other. Ecstasy broke down class barriers, we liked to think. Conversations could be begun easily with anyone, always starting with the intimate murmur of, "All right?" and that special E grin. Nor were the clubs pick-up joints. For a while we weren't even that interested in sex. It was more fun to see the night out together, all going back to someone's place to talk and chill with decks and spliff instead.' i

Often in the week, I would be outside somewhere like The Wag Club in Soho, The Limelight in Shaftesbury Avenue, Brixton Academy or The Fridge at 3am, handing out fliers for our club night, as people were leaving. Sometimes I'd flyer a queue of people waiting to get in to a club. No mobiles, no internet … this is how word got about.

> *Breath. Pause. Feelings moving in my body: gratitude and joy for this written opportunity to create a shape of my experience. Sadness too, in all that is missed. I grieve what is not remembered and unsaid.*

Transpersonal Psychotherapy

The story resumes: I am aged 26 or 27. Music, dancing and club promotion are first and forefront, but I am aware that this may not be my path into my 30s. I begin my own psychotherapy as a pre-requisite for Psychotherapy training. Aged 28 my 5-year journey into training as a Transpersonal Psychotherapist begins. The Transpersonal approach is partly based on the work of Carl Jung and embraces a spiritual approach to human development. I am the product of my parents: the

Mind is the powerhouse and I have a hunger to learn. I am also the product of my environment: the rhythms of multiculturalism, music, dance. I have my own soul yearnings: to move widely and deeply in this world.

> *There are tears in my eyes. I drop my attention further into my breath, deeper into my body. This is feeling like a nature memoir where every nook and cranny of the landscape, every flutter of insect wing is recorded. Here the nature of the landscape is me, and dancing is the ground, the air, the big horizon. I shift between a need to carefully excavate and document the story and a horror that it is being told.*

Caribbean Carnival

I have the opportunity to go to Antigua for Carnival, a 10-day exuberant celebration, marking the end of slavery on the Caribbean island in 1834. I have partied many times at London's Notting Hill Carnival, and this is not so very different. Floats, costumes, pageantry, Calypso Soca, reggae, steel bands, sound systems. Everyone gets up really early on the first day of this carnival: people take to the streets at 4 am for 'J'Ouvert'(meaning daybreak) The party begins… and the crowd went wild.

More sensory memory:

> *it's night-time. My Rasta friend and I are heading into St John's, the capital city, carnival zone. We can hear the sound of heavy reggae beats, a man on the mic 'toasting' (talking to the crowds as they dance). People everywhere and it's dark. The light of cooking in stalls selling jerk chicken, other morsels, the smoke wafting into the warm Caribbean air. The smell of good food.*

> *Again, a perimeter fence, made of palm leaves or something else. Inside it's heaving and it's all bass. The crowd are deep*

into the dance; there are whistles and shouts. Rough terrain underfoot, you can feel the music coming up through the earth. Sometimes there's a pause in the music; the DJ will play a tune again, rewind, and maybe again, rewind; the crowd explodes with anticipation. Every so often the sound of gunshot goes off in keeping with the explosive and euphoric mood. In moments, I feel the bass inside my body, organs reverberating. It's edgy and irresistible. My feet keep moving.

Altered States

As I moved further into my therapy training, I learnt about altered states, hylotropic breathwork, expanded states of consciousness, peak experiences, the dissolving of the ego and transpersonal (beyond the personal) states of being. I was still partying and intrigued by the parallels of what I was discovering in the therapy world and what I was experiencing on the dancefloor.

Whilst the rave scene was fuelled by drugs, in particular 'Ecstasy' (MDMA), I also knew that what I was witnessing - the feeling of deep connection and belonging - was real and clearly compelling for thousands of people. I was of the view that just because drugs were involved, the experience did not lack meaning. I wanted to know if this feeling of unity and bonding could happen without the drugs particularly as stories were emerging of people who had died from hyperthermia and dehydration whilst raving and taking Ecstasy.

Spirit in the House

I devised a therapeutic workshop 'Spirit in the House' to investigate the rave phenomenon in a non-drug setting. There was guided meditation, drawing, and participants were invited to bring along music that they had enjoyed whilst out raving. We danced to each other's tracks and then discussed the experience. The media loved it, and I ended up in the Sunday papers! A psychotherapist who was interested in the rave scene; they thought it was funny, even scandalous.

One journalist, Oliver Bennett, interviewed me for the Independent on Sunday in December 1996. He described '...*that alienated end-of-disco-feeling*' and how I was offering an antidote in the form of '*post-fun stress counselling*'. He summarised my aim for the Spirit in the House workshops:

> '*For [Franks]... rave is not just lurching around on drugs in time to metronomic music, but an expression of "shared vision", a "sense of community", and a way of "accessing deeper meaning in people's lives".*' ii

I hooked up with Nick Saunders, writer of E is for Ecstasy. We gave a talk at Neal's Yard, Covent Garden about the value of the rave experience: the feelings of unity on the dancefloor, across cultural, class, gender identity and sexuality boundaries.

I began to move away from the club and rave world. I no longer wanted to stay up all night and the drugs didn't interest me. My attention was now aligned with personal growth and consciousness. Little did I know that these raving years would have such reach and meaning for my work in the decades to come.

> *I re-route my attention, away from story-telling and memory-mining. Arms retracted from keyboard. I notice the sensation of my forefinger and thumb pressing together. I notice the warmth, the pressure, a sensory connection. My awareness shuttles between the movements of my mind, the sensations of my body and fragments of feeling.*

Process work

It's the 1990s and I am knee high in the therapy training world. Here I encountered the work of Arnold Mindell, a Jungian analyst and founder of

Process Work. His key idea was the 'dreambody' which connects body experiences and sensations with dreams. He said that we are dreaming not only when we are asleep but also when we are awake, and one way we can pay attention to this is through exploring our body symptoms. The reason we do this is that there are powerful messages for oneself and the collective here, and that this is where new and creative ideas can emerge.iii

For me it was a homecoming: here was a powerful system of transformation (for individuals and groups) that followed nonverbal communication. Body-orientated, respectful of feelings, playful, intelligent. Process Work spoke to me loud and clear. I could use awareness of the body and movement – things that I was instinctively drawn to – to offer something meaningful and potent in my therapy work.

Finally I could see and know that the wisdom of the body and wisdom of the mind were one.

> *I can feel a wide and expansive landscape, in my limbs, my breath. I am scared. I contract. There are large parts of the culture that I swim in that do not and will not except what I am saying. I must keep swimming.*

Raising a family

I tread water for some years: marriage, children, family life. My work moves to the UK National Health Service (NHS) where I have a pastoral role in an inner-city Sexual Health service. I leave behind my interest in the world of the moving body. My attention is elsewhere.

My dance has gone quiet. And yet it doesn't go away.

Family life meant tiredness, becoming more health conscious, wanting to go to bed earlier to be up with the larks for the kids. My pull towards the dancefloor hadn't gone away. It was just waiting for the time and setting to come back to life.

Conscious Movement

As I started to get energy back from the hard child-rearing years, I turned towards 'Conscious Movement/Dance' or Movement Meditation, embodied practice that offered sober dancing with awareness in the body and breath. Yoga was great, Tai Chi was cool, but nothing could beat the feelings of freedom on a dancefloor, the joy of moving to music.

I was initially a little sceptical about whether this wholistic dancing could have any of the edge and vibrancy of a sweaty rave or club. I was also 15 years older than in my night club heyday, and uncertain how my middle-aged self (both in body and spirit) could find the gratification and euphoria of my youth on the dancefloor.

Unlike for many other people, it wasn't the sober aspect of conscious dance that presented a challenge. I had partied and raved very often on one or maybe 2 beers; I liked being the driver amongst friends. It was the music side of things that bothered me. In my younger days I was accustomed to being around people with very honed musical tastes. I loved the music we endlessly listened and danced to, at parties, clubs, festivals, raves. I found it hard to believe that this passion could be reproduced in this conscious dance context.

I was wrong. I went to my first 5Rhythms (5R) session about 15 years ago and have never wanted to stop. Sometimes during a session – the rhythms of Staccato or Chaos, it has felt EXACTLY like being at a club or rave. Wild abandon is everywhere. I also liked the pauses in 5R dance; there was a chance to rest and recover. To breathe and relax, before the next wave of movement got going. I had found an important jigsaw piece in my life map.

Diary of a conscious dance teacher, Monday

I'm going for a jog in the park. Good start to the week. I put on my Spotify 'Discover Weekly', the smart algorithm of music based on what I've been listening to.

Something joyful inside. An upward shooting feeling in my stomach, my chest. Music that I love. The uplifting feeling of the beat, the rhythm. A welcome reprieve from preoccupying, normal reality.

I put in my EarPods before leaving the house. Allured by the beat, I find myself in some funky hallway dance. The beat's so compelling, the streets less so.

Some days, as I peruse the algorithm it seems that a lot of tracks are a good match. I light up. I can see and feel them on the dancefloor. Other times Siri is hard at work moving the tracks on in search of some gold. Again, I wonder is this my mood or has the technology not quite hit the spot this week.

The dance of Saturday's Flomotion dance session is still reverberating in my system. Part of me wants to dissect the experience; to minutely track each moment to distil what went well, to eliminate what didn't. No, impossible! Lived experience tells me that's not the way to go. Each session is a bit different for many unknown reasons.

I lightly save a few ideas for tweaking the sessions going forward.

Groups and Dynamics

My work as a Psychotherapist flourished. I had resisted committing myself to the field for some years. I couldn't find a way to bring the wisdom of the body into the therapy room. With the help of a supervisor familiar with Process Work, I was able to bring a sense of aliveness into the therapy room that aligned with my experience and values.

Something in me is a bit shut down. I notice my mouth is clenched. The words are not flowing. Take a deep breath. Give myself some space. I can feel my story hurtling towards the present. I am scared I will reach the end and something important will remain untold. I re-invite myself into body sensation. Drop the project. Be.

My interest developed in working with groups. I started to run a weekly dance session despite being scared and intimidated by being the one in charge, the visible one, the one talking whilst others listened to my instructions. The evenings were small and intimate, unpolished but full of warmth and soul. I played the music that I grew up listening and dancing to: soul, funk, reggae, house, Latin, African beats, Samba, disco and more. There was also time for rest, relaxation and meditation in the session.

I did a Teacher Training course in Ecstatic Awakening Dance. I had gained so much from my dance practice; I was certain I had something to offer others in this sphere. The crossover with therapy was evident: body awareness offers the opportunity to explore our life patterns (of thinking, of feeling, of relating) both on and off the dancefloor.

Online dance

Covid 19 arrived, I was no longer able to run in-person dance. I moved online to weekly Zoom classes. These are well-attended. People were stuck in their homes and longing for connection, community, exercise and the opportunity to dance. Flomotion was born at this time: a fusion of the sounds of my London nightlife, various conscious dance practices (Ecstatic Dance, 5Rhythms, Open Floor), Spirit in the House, Process Work and the accumulation of therapeutic work spanning my adult lifetime.

Flomotion emerged from lockdown to its present home, a Saturday night in Archway, North London, and monthly online sessions with other offers in the pipeline.

I sit back. I am still. Breath is even. I have traced a path and arrived somewhere. This isn't the end. This is a moment. My ribs hold steady, uncertain whether to breath a big sigh of relief or to wait for what's to come. I wait.

This is something personal. It was in these lockdown times that my father's Parkinson's disease got significantly worse. Later in the book I will say more about how dance can address isolation and conditions like Parkinson's, but let me tell you something about dancing with my 90 year old dad. I knew that having to be at home alone would not be good for him. Once we were allowed to form a bubble, I suggested that we dance together; I would make a playlist of his favourite music or tracks he would enjoy dancing to. The results were extraordinary. After 15-20 minutes of dancing, he was considerably more focused, his balance was better; he was more like himself before the Parkinson's. All the research says dance is very helpful for Parkinson's. I witnessed this directly in my dear father.

Diary of a Conscious dance teacher, Tuesday

I receive an email from a regular dancer on the Flomotion floor. She's unwell. Missing the dance. I am sad. She is a wonderful woman, loved by many. We have been dancing together for some years. Her signature on the dancefloor is graceful, rhythmic.

We don't know a lot about each other's lives and yet we know each other intimately. Messages are exchanged with love and the longing to be reunited again in moves and grooves.

On the dancefloor we create threads of connection, finding ways and patterns to reach each other, to reach ourselves. Over and over. Again and again.

At the session this week, there were several new people and few less of the 'regulars' on the dancefloor. When this happens, I tend to provide a bit more guidance, give the session more shape in order to communicate safety and *encouragement. This week, I moved the playlist around and guided some group movement to bring energy and focus back to the present. It seemed to work; people who entered shy and inhibited, began to take up space on the dancefloor.*

I was deeply heartened by one dancer, returning for his second dance, who had been very shut down and could barely move on his first session. This time his movements were bolder, he was able to make some eye contact, and his whole demeanour was relaxed and available. I have seen this many times; some people need more sessions to release themselves, others less. It is deeply fulfilling.

I want to dance with somebody

In her book, Dance Your Way Home, Emma Warren says that 'we dance our histories directly and indirectly...we belong to ways of moving that are rooted in location, lineage, self-image and family.'

Catch me on the dance floor and the story I have told on these pages will be there in my steps, my bends, the way my body swirls and the way breath moves through me. This is my body's account of my story. And then I encounter yours!

Many years of lived experience spanning the world of healing and the mood of party have led to the words that now roll out on these pages. It has also meant that I have a wide catalogue of music reflective of multicultural London that has been my home since birth.

My hope and offer of this book is that it moves you: emotionally, intellectually, relationally, spiritually and predominantly physically, preferably towards a dancing space with others. By drawing on history, science, music, literature, psychotherapy, dance theory, lived experience, over 40 years on the dance and more, I want to invite you into a world that begins at the beginning of life with our heartbeat, to a world that can, and does support people to live more fulfilled, connected and joyful lives.

In the next chapter we look at dance being a birth right; not just an add-on, something to do if time allows. For many millennia in the West it was taken away, and it seems this had massive consequences both for collective identity and individual mental health. We now understand a lot more about the biomechanics and emotional hinterland of human life and this is where it points: If you want to live, you need to dance!

In the mid-eighties, electronic dance music with high bpm and euphoric melody lines transformed clubbing, and new spaces, 'raves', drew together musicians, entrepreneurs, visual artists and, of course, young people (and some not so young) who leaped at this opportunity to dance free style in a hot, loud atmosphere where illegal drugs outsold alcohol.

> I still consider myself so lucky to have had a friend who was in on all this and could take me to events which changed me. I loved the sensation of uplift from a crowd which suddenly (on a good night) melded into one consciousness as the atmosphere 'kicked' and the music and its effects in the body became the whole of everything. I loved feeling my internal organs vibrating with the bass and the sweat running down my arms. I loved it when lively boys came along to encourage a flagging dancer and with a huge smile bring them back into the community of the rhythm.
>
> But what is an old raver to do when time moves on? Basically, allow the body's memories to live and find someone like Julia to curate a playlist and create a community – a place once more where a group can seek the connection of dance, and honour a more mature understanding of the emotions it may release.
>
> Maria Gayton

I was shy and retiring in late teens and early 20s and would only dance if really drunk. When you are older, you don't care what peers are thinking, although I feel it more in my knees. When I first went to 5R, I went into a corner trying not to be noticed. I have natural rhythms that draw people in.

There hadn't been a lot of space for dancing in my life partly because I got my movement enjoyment though things like Tai Chi. It's incredible to be able move your body in time to music; once you 'get it' it feels good, and you feel alive. It tests your body, and you know what your body can do.

It's nice to meet other people in the class who can keep the rhythm with you; it's communication like a good conversation. I love it when all the 'old faces' turn up; no expectations, have a laugh. Once you are relaxed the movement comes easy.

George Burgess

TWO

The Origins of Dance and Human Evolution

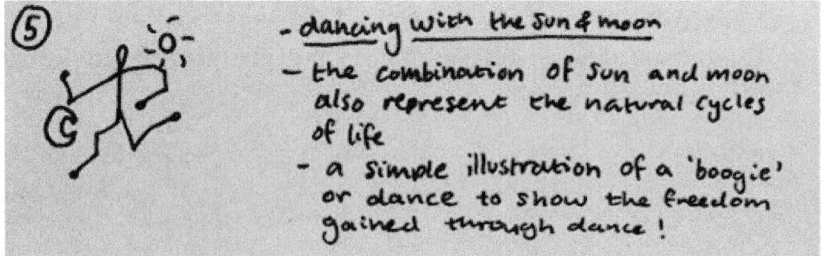

Dancing is your birthright.

Heartbeat. The sound of our mothers' heartbeat in utero. The first rhythm, deeply embedded in the foetal human body. The eternal soundtrack of our lives. The awakening of life from within our bodies. Our heartbeat accelerates when we feel happy, contracts when we feel sad, in fact it reacts with lightning speed to changes in our body and emotions.

Babies and toddlers can move to a beat. Rhythm and dance are deeply embedded in our individual and collective DNA. All people in all times in all places have engaged in dance. The intelligence of life is cast in our bodies. Releasing ourselves to the beat; bodies in synchrony as we find movement, and the beat moves us.

'Once your body surrenders to movement, your soul remembers its dance.' Gabriel Roth, Sweat Your Prayers

The Dancing Universe

'Dance is the movement of the universe concentrated in an individual.' Isadora Duncan

According to Indian tradition, the Universe is continuously in motion; a dance symbolised by the great God, Shiva, the Cosmic Dancer, associated with creation and destruction, and the never-ending cycle of time. The Universe is endlessly renewing itself; everything is a dance.

'This idea contains an implicit message: However precarious, isolated, or desperate you may feel your existence to be, you are nevertheless taking part in the dance; and you are part of a universe that is fundamentally all right. The message then becomes more specific: It you want to perceive the deepest aspects of this reality, you must dance.' Piero Ferrucci (Inevitable Grace)

As well as Shiva in India, many other ancient peoples and cultures understood the important link between dancing and health: in ancient Greece, Apollo was the god of dance, music and healing. Others include the Egyptian goddess Bas (or Bastet) and Baal the semitic god.

Ferruci quotes great dancers who say that dance is 'a return to our primordial origins'. It connects us 'with energy in its pure form, with the gods at the time of creation'. The Roman poet Lucian wrote that *'the movements of the stars reflect the original dance of the universe.'*

'In its highest and most beautiful forms, dance is the activity of

the gods: light, carefree celebration of life. Those who dance are not working, are not imprisoned by daily routine, and are free from the usual pain and worry. Dance reminds us of a lost world or a world we have long yearned for; it is the ideal representation of the unimaginable joy we glimpse only in our moments of greatest happiness.' Ferruci

Ekhart Tolle, spiritual teacher and best-selling author, said *'life is the dancer, and you are the dance'*.

Human bonding and evolution

Dancing has been very important in the evolution of humanity, in particular for our ability to bond and collaborate. It has been a significant, and predominantly overlooked factor in the success of humans becoming the dominant species on the planet. We have not been the biggest, most dominant animal on the scene, but we worked out how to cooperate with one another and dancing was in the glue.

Here's two neuroscientists on the subject:

'This community feeling is rooted in our evolutionary past, and is, therefore, deeply embedded in each of us…Group bonding became necessary for survival. Rituals and traditions evolved to reinforce these bonds…All cultures, all over the world, developed groups dances. Today science shows that moving together in synchrony to music or to a particular rhythm was very important for the evolution and development of human societies. Dancing strengthened the social bonds within a group and gave people a feeling of identity and belonging…' (Dancing is the Best Medicine) Julia F. Christensen and Dong-Seon Chang

Professor William H McNeill, described as 'one of our greatest living historians', authored a book, <u>Moving Together in Time</u>, after his conscription to the US army in 1941. Months of marching in the drill field with other men led him to realise that the *'muscular bonding'* this experience induced was sublimely releasing of his individual sense of self in favour of becoming part of the whole.

Later in life, using this experience and his encyclopaedic knowledge of human evolution he concluded that the quantum shift of human culture on earth, 40,000 years ago, was the arrival of language as a way of reacting to the external world. He identifies that prior to fully developed language there would have been...

> *'cruder ways of communicating... using something like pidgin at the verbal level, backed up with shared emotional solidarities induced by dance.'*

Dance, community, language.

Here we encounter the synchrony of dance as pivotal in the evolution of humanity with its ability to strengthen emotional bonds, permitting mutual protection, territorial ownership, the search for and sharing of food and nurturance of the young. This was all made possible because of dancing together and the cooperation it provided therein. Dance made human language feasible.

> *'Underneath it all we are tribal individuals. We seek connection because we need to know we are not alone on this planet.'*
> (Sweat Your Prayers) Gabriel Roth

In her excellent book, Barbara Ehrenreich (Dancing in the Streets) takes this further. She says that whilst language was crucial for bonding humans in groups so important for survival, it was in fact music and dancing that was needed to bind people into communities. Ehrenreich investigates why ecstatic rituals, once so prevalent and pivotal to human evolution, are not commonly available. She traces dancing back to prehistoric times around the world. She makes the point:

'Clearly, danced rituals did not seem like a waste of energy to prehistoric peoples. They took the time to fashion masks and costumes; they wontly expended calories in the execution of the dance; they preferred to record these scenes over any other group activity'. She makes the point that 'when nature requires us to do something...it kindly rewires our brains to make that activity enjoyable...the joy of the rhythmic activity [of dance] would have helped overcome the fear of confronting predators and other threats...'

Crossing an evolutionary threshold

Jonathan Haidt, a social psychologist, describes humans as *'the only ultrasocial primate'*; in evolutionary terms this means that we crossed a threshold from selfish individualism to live in large groups with structure to reap the benefits as described above – food, defended territory, division of labour.

Haidt says the first step to ultra-sociality was the ability to share intentions in groups of hunters/foragers, in other words to collaborate, which he dates to 600,000 or 700,000 years ago. It took a further several hundred thousand years for bigger and more complex collaborative groups of three thousand people. The most successful groups were the most cohesive, conforming to social norms, sharing group emotions, creating and abiding by social (and religious) institutions. Haidt argues that genes coevolved with these cultural developments putting group as well as individual selection on the evolutionary map.

In this context, one can see that forms of group bonding are crucial for the survival and dominance of early humans. Haidt draws on the work of O'Neill and Ehrenreich for understanding of what he describes as the *'groupish overlay'* or *'hive switch'* that humans can manifest when they are not in *'relentless competition'*, one individual against another. Here, he says, dance is the path into collaborative co-existence.

The Hive Switch

Jonathan Haidt developed The Hive Hypothesis. He tells us that human nature is '90 per cent chimp' (we are primates with brains shaped by a competitive nature for our survival) but that we are also '10 per cent bee' in that we are highly social and have evolved from groups that managed to bond, cooperate, and ultimately out-competed other groups. He says that under certain conditions we were able to transcend our self-interest and 'lose ourselves (temporarily and ecstatically) in something larger than ourselves'. This is what he calls The Hive Switch. There are many ways to switch the hive switch on; he names 'raves' as one such way.

When we dance with others, we lose a sense of isolation, a body whose skin is the boundary between ourselves and 'the other'. We feel connected without the need for verbal communication and sharing the details of our lives. There is no hierarchy and status present in the movement. Just bodies moving, feeling, sharing and connecting.

Dance and religion

Dance is mentioned 21-27 times in the Bible depending on the translation used, and the mystical expression of both Islam (Sufism) and Judaism (Hasidism) both contain ecstatic practices. Shamanism, a religious practice where a shaman interacts with the spirit world often in an altered state of consciousness offering healing and divination, is associated with tribal and indigenous cultures. Rhythmic drumming and dancing are central to the Shaman's transition into this trance or altered state.

Old Dancing Gods

There is evidence that the ancient Hebrews and Greeks all participated in ecstatic ritual behaviour. The Greek god of wine Dionysus (Bacchus to the Romans) was the quintessential raver with devotees dancing themselves into a state of trance. There was also the horned god, Pan, who presided over dance and ecstatic states. Women were particular devotees of Dionysus, with written accounts from the second century CE of organised ecstatic events for female worshippers, and madness and violence imposed on non-participants. Gods resembling Dionysus appeared in numerous locations including North Africa and India.

Ehrenreich tells us that as societies evolved, so did social hierarchies and elites with their need for military defence. Ecstatic rituals were curtailed in order to avoid the equalising effect and the threat to the status quo. The activities of poor and marginalised groups (including women) were suppressed. In Ancient Greece, ecstatic ritual went underground performed only by the ruling elite (men), whilst the Romans stamped out traditional collective activity altogether.

Jesus arrives on the scene. This marks the acceleration of monotheism, although in the first and second centuries CE, before 'Western' thought takes hold, there was some compatibility and overlap between early Christianity and ecstatic religious cults, with some quarters offering singing, chanting, speaking in tongues and dancing culminating in ecstatic states. By the end of the first century, Christianity started to create hierarchies and formal officers (bishops and deacons) and in the early fourth century Christianity had become the official religion of Rome.

No Dancing in Church!

By the middle of the fourth century, religious dancing - especially by women and especially of an ecstatic nature - was outlawed by the Church. Having a hotline to divine knowledge through ecstatic revelations was not compatible with or desirable for the established order.

Nonetheless, into the late Middle Ages, dancing in churches was commonplace, though by the end of the thirteenth century this behaviour had been stamped out.

Unable to wipe out this ecstatic behaviour altogether, the Church permitted festivities of drinking, dancing and play outside of churches on special Church holidays, a move that *'helped to shape European culture for centuries'* (Ehrenreich). In the thirteenth century, there was an expansion in carnival festivities. However, heretical movements in parts of Europe threatened to splinter the Catholic Church and consequently in 1233 the Church introduced the papal Inquisition for the suppression of heresy. Celebrations, dance manias and other festivities continued unabated throughout the middle ages, just not inside churches.

There was a secularizing effect of excluding carnival activities from the church. Ecstatic states were no longer associated with god-worshipping, but rather confirmed as an experience entirely made by humans, enjoyed by humans. God had officially left the party, but the party persisted in the form of many holy days of outdoor festivities plus weddings, wakes and other local celebrations. Work was forbidden and uplifting celebration was tolerated and enjoyed by many.

All work, no dance

During the sixteenth to the nineteenth century in the northern Christian world, Church and state put an end to carnival activity and ecstatic experience articulated in thousands of acts of legislation banning festivities. Here's Ehrenreich:

> *'The loss, to ordinary people, of so many recreations and festivities is incalculable; and we, who live in a culture of almost devoid of opportunities either to "lose ourselves" in communal festivities or to distinguish ourselves in any arena outside of work, are in no position to fathom it.'*

The emergence of capitalism with its emphasis on hard work and profit-making, the rise of Calvinist Protestantism which encouraged hard work and avoiding sinfulness, along with a disillusionment with the material excesses of the Catholic Church and the old feudal nobility, put a nail in the coffin of the communal merry-making and a growth towards uninterrupted work time. Max Weber wrote: *'The most urgent task [of Calvinism was] the destruction of spontaneous, impulsive enjoyment.'* (The Protestant Ethic and the Spirit of Capitalism).

From the late sixteenth century on, carnival developed a more political, anti-establishment tone that authorities were keen to quell. Population rises in Europe, a dispersal of displaced peasants, rising prices and falling wages, increased urbanization and industrialisation created an underclass of poverty-stricken people. Public cavorting was seen as potentially revolutionary, especially after the arrival of guns at carnival in the latter part of the sixteenth century.

Even in the sphere of warfare, rank and file soldiers were *'forcibly restrained from the drinking and carousing that had once enlivened military service for so many reluctant conscripts'* and the move to gun-based warfare required huge numbers of soldiers into *'obedience and self-denial'*. Ehrenreich.

Melancholy, loneliness, and the emergent 'self'

The work ethic had set in. Group enjoyment was on the decline. Loneliness and isolation on the rise and ultimately huge amounts of depression, described as 'melancholy' spread throughout Europe. Historians have noted that at this time (c 1600s) there was a psychological shift in Europe towards the individual 'self' rather than a collective 'we'. This was accompanied by a preoccupation with the opinion and perceived judgements of others which fuelled the inevitable rise of anxiety.

Ehrenreich makes the point:

'Nothing speaks more clearly of the darkening mood, the

declining possibilities for joy, than the fact that, while the medieval peasant created festivities as an escape from work, the Puritan embraced work as an escape from terror.'

However, she counsels caution in blaming the end of ecstatic festivities for the rise in depression whilst also citing many international examples throughout history that do indeed point to communal merrymaking as a cure for it.

Colonialisation and Empire

If the removal of collective joy wasn't bad enough in European society, the story gets worse in the 400 year era of imperialism, colonialisation and slavery, as European explorers and missionaries travelled the world to exploit and control the people and resources of other places. There were repeated attempts to suppress the culture of indigenous peoples with particular emphasis on dismantling communal rites and rituals including and especially dancing. Of course, it was not only the communal joy that was killed off; tragically and sickeningly it is estimated that 50 million people were killed in the colonial genocide.

Collective effervescence

Emile Durkheim, the influential sociologist, coined the term '*collective effervescence*'. He noted that people operate at two levels: as an individual which binds one person to another, and at a collective level, relevant to the experience of dancing together in groups:

'The second are those which bind me to the social entity as a whole; these manifest themselves primarily in the relationships of the society with other societies, and could be called "intersocial." The first [set of emotions] leave[s] my autonomy and personality almost intact. No doubt they tie me to others, but without taking much of my independence from me. When I act under the influence of the second, by contrast, I am simply a

part of the whole, whose actions I follow, and whose influence I am subject to.'

It is in this second sense, at a community or society level, that collective effervescence can occur with its intense, passionate, powerful and unifying emotions. Durkheim regarded this as the realm of the sacred. Jonathan Haidt identifies collective effervescence as being akin to the hive switch that we met earlier in this chapter.

Here I think of the mass dances of the rave scene, festivals, carnival, clubs and conscious dance, where everyone is sharing the vibe and exchanging energy. This must be something akin to the festive dancing of our forebears and dancing people of indigenous cultures.

Diary of a Conscious Dance Teacher Wednesday

This morning I have been reading the news. The human world is a big mess.

Two devastating wars, displaced people through climate emergency, child poverty, ecological breakdown and the list goes on. I wonder about my privileged enclave in North London. What has all this dancing got to do, if anything, with the suffering that is going on around the world? I have no answers. I can remain aware and open, making change where I can, connecting with others, being humble, following what life seems to be teaching me.

I tinker again with the playlist. What was I thinking of putting that track there? No way. I have to feel my way back in. Re-enter the emotional, sensate slipstream. This requires something slower, more embodied than how my functional life plays out.

I often say compiling the playlist is like cooking: you need some crunch here, some spice there, something creamy. There's texture and colour to consider. Variation and *contrast. There's also something cultural for me. I want to travel the world with the sounds and moves, mix it up. This is the multicultural landscape that has been background for my whole life. I can bring it into the foreground and celebrate it in the dance space.*

Open Floor training has taught me that transitions are very important. As we move from one part of the dance to the other, I need some spaces of no music or instrumental to allow me to speak, make contact with the group, to guide them from one part of the session to another. I now have a genre and playlist called 'After Inner Dance': not too fast, no vocals, a tangible beat. I receive feedback, watch the crowd and learn about what they need. I pick tracks accordingly and find words of encouragement.

This evening me and my husband will be going to dance 5R with Liz Baron Cohen in Paddington. We've been dancing with Liz on and off for about 10 years. I can't wait: so much of my development and learning about dance has happened in the big gymnasium at Paddington College.

Embodied Brain

In the last few decades, neuroscience has established the firm connection of mind and body as one interdependent intelligence system, and that the brain is a social organ, constantly adapting and modifying itself to lived experience.

We now know that the human brain is connected to every part of the body via the nervous system which dictates and coordinates every action of the human body. The purpose of the brain is to process information. Sensory neurons (cells) receive information from the senses (the body), and motor neurons (cells) send out electrical impulses for action to take place. 90% of this activity operates at an unconscious level; we don't 'think' about this, it happens beneath awareness, and it is happening all the time. Information is constantly being collected from the world around us, and from the world inside us (eg muscle activity, gut health and breathing).

We also know that when we dance, neurotransmitters (chemical 'messengers' that transmit information from one neuron to another) are activated. These include dopamine (pleasure/reward system), serotonin (promotes feelings of wellbeing), endorphins (suppress pain) and oxytocin (creates feelings of closeness to others).

Affective neuroscience, the study of how the brain processes emotions, is a field that is evolving as we gain more understanding of how the brain functions. Importantly it is now understood that healthy relationships are fundamental and necessary for the evolution of the contemporary human brain, and this takes place via our social engagement system, rather than when the survival system of threat and defence are activated.

This is hugely relevant for conscious dance practice in providing the kind of setting of safety our systems need to be present, to engage and to connect. It also informs us about what is happening in our brains when we connect through movement, and how we can use this information to create trusting and growthful relationships based on empathy and compassion.

My thanks here goes to Caitriona Nic Ghiollaphadraig, herself a teacher of Open Floor Movement practice who educates other teachers in this field about neuroscience and how this is important for our work.

Here's Ferrucci again:

> *'Dance is not a private event occurring only in the dancer's body. Dancing is public. Spectators participate empathically and they too feel the lightness of dance. They behold a world of grace and harmony, and understand that they have been*

allowed to take part in it. That is why audiences can be so enthusiastic and grateful towards great dancers'.

Mirror and Resonance systems

Social or Affective neuroscience tells us about mirror and resonance circuitry in the brain that is highly relevant for understanding the power of movement and dance. Resonance behaviours are reflexive imitation responses we make when we interact with other people, which may well have evolved to coordinate group behaviour for gathering, hunting, fight/flight and migrating. Mirror neurons activate both when we witness others engage in functional behaviours or when we ourselves engage in these actions; they are probably connected to many social functions including learning, empathy, verbal and non-verbal communication.

> *'Mirror neurons…lie at the crossroads of inner and outer experience, where multiple networks of visual, motor, and emotional processing converge (Iacoboni et al., 2011). It is because of their privileged position that mirror neurons are able to bridge observation and action. These systems contain maps of other people and the space around us, as well as our own musculature, survival needs and strategies for attaining goals. Over the past 20 years, mirror systems have helped us to understand how our brains link together in the synchronisation of such group behaviours as hunting, dancing, and emotional attunement (Jeannerod, 2001).'*
>
> Louis Cozolino, *The Neuroscience of Human Relationships*

Music

You could say that without music there is no dance, so let's give music some attention.

Like dance, there has been music throughout human history. There is evidence of basic musical instruments dating back to 35-40,000 years ago. The first music was probably the human voice when prehistoric people imitated the sounds of nature for religious and recreational purposes. Every culture has music and although the exact origins of music are not agreed on, most cultures have their own myths concerning the origins of music.

The ancient Greeks had their own system of music, as did Jewish people for religious purposes. The Vedas, the sacred Hindu books, have information about classical Indian Music, and ancient music flourished in the Persian Empire and in Egypt. Music continued to develop and broaden in the Medieval and Renaissance eras, right up to the present day.

The compelling story of music is the same as dance: it has the capacity to engage and inspire human emotions. Music directly affects our brain. Here's two neuroscientist on the subject:

> *'Music is an enormous stimulation for our brain. Countless studies have proven that it impacts our hormonal balance and decreases stress more effectively than any medication. Music also enhances our power of concentration and our emotional and linguistic competence…above all, music makes us happy because it offers us a whole cocktail of the so-called happiness hormones. It puts us into a good mood and lets us forget that we are actually working hard when we dance'*. Christensen and Chang.

It Turns Out We're Born to Groove

So revealed the extensive work of Henkjan Honing at the prestigious Massachusetts Institute of Technology (MIT) in which he demonstrated 'unequivocally' that motor and auditory parts of the brain are strongly wired in humans compared to nonhuman primates. He states:

'music is not solely a cultural phenomenon but also possesses deep biological roots, apparently offering an evolutionary advantage to our species.' iv

Sounding familiar? Modern research and understanding of music, or 'musicality' (our innate capacity for music), is indicating a similar story to that of dance and the role it has played in human evolution and predominance. If we are hardwired to respond to music and beat, moving our bodies in dance is a natural outcome and a valuable advantage.

This is What Music Sounds Like is the fascinating book by award-winning professor of cognitive neuroscientist, Dr Susan Rogers and mathematical neuroscientist, Dr Ogi Ogden in which they invite readers to discover their 'listener profile' and 'what the music you love says about you'. They outline neural networks that the link our auditory and motor systems, and how these contribute to social communication. On rhythm they say:

'Dancing is the most common and pleasurable way for humans to express their love of rhythm...The human affection for dancing has prompted many music scientists to declare that we cannot truly understand our relationship with music unless we consider how music makes us move.'

> Stepping onto a dancefloor filled with other moving bodies is like diving into a cool swimming pond. I feel contained by a space crackling with aliveness. It's an opportunity to tune into myself – what sensations are going on for me right now, where am I feeling this in my body? – and also to experience the energy of being with others. I have the opportunity to play with 'me', then play with 'we', and to enjoy the musicality that bubbles within me and around me. I relish the connection; on a plane I don't often experience in everyday life.

Yearning for and reclaiming the birth right.

In this chapter we've travelled far, and our movement has been expansive and far-reaching. We've taken big steps back to the dawn of time itself, the beginning of the universe, and discovered dance there. We've touched into the human heartbeat, the enduring soundscape of our entire mortal lives. We've seen how our ability to move together in time created the muscular bonding that was the forerunner to language as our primary tool of communication, our collaboration and ultimately to the dominance of our species on this planet.

Also in this chapter, we have seen how before the Christian era, the dancing path was well- trodden by ancient peoples, but around 1600 CE in the Western world, religious and political factors snuffed out the party. Moving into the contemporary era, we learnt about dancing and neuroscience, why dance is so compelling for the human race, and about how the power of music (like dance) has the capacity to engage emotions and is hard-wired into us from birth unlike any other species.

In the next chapter we will look at the popularisation of dance since the 1960s around the world and in particular how conscious movement developed. We will look at up to date understandings of our nervous system and trauma, and how this relates to the moving body.

> In our culture, spaces where we can be with others without talking are rare. To dance in such a space brings me a feeling of relief and freedom, especially when it's led by someone who embodies authenticity and is highly skilled at creating a sense of safety.
>
> There's a relaxing of my usual patterns of protection and defence, allowing a connection with the other dancers that goes much deeper than I find possible in normal social situations. This creates a sense of true community

and belonging for me. There's something so joyful and healing about being witnessed without judgement and dancing in the presence of others in this way.

Amanda Penalver

> I have been dancing for about 17 years, since my friend Julia introduced me to 5 Rhythms. Before this I couldn't dance. I was too wooden, restricted and shy. Little did I realise before the age of 36 that dancing would become such an integral part of my life, creative expression and heart.

Since then, I find dance releases tension and it is brilliant to dance before doing a big presentation or running an event. It just loosens everything up, both physically and mentally. When creating an event or project I dance first, during and after! Dancing brings my work into pure flow. It removes the potential of overthinking, allowing physical embodiment of my art in the world.

Dancing helps me to feel connected, in touch with my body and free. When I am dancing, I am centred, and old patterns and worries feel manageable. When I dance I am in touch with the essence of life which brings everything into perspective. Dancing has also supported me along the peri-menopause journey, relieving a great deal of exhaustion and pain. Dance helped me to re-connect with my energy. It's joyous too. Especially when a track I really resonate with comes on!

Emily Love

THREE

The Rediscovery of Dance

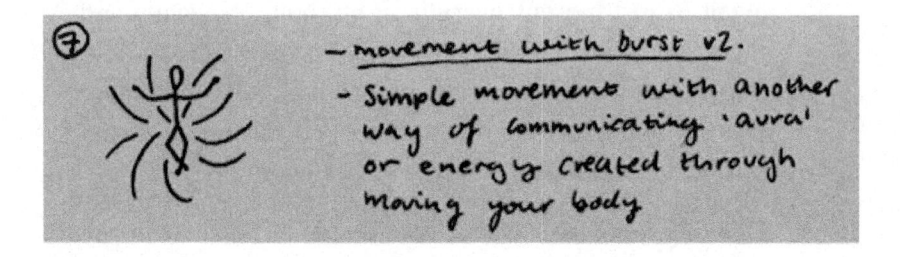

> — movement with burst v2.
> - Simple movement with another way of communicating 'aura' or energy created through moving your body

The Age of Aquarius

A song from the 1967 musical, Hair, captured the zeitgeist of the 1960s and 1970s. It spoke of 'The Dawning of the Age of Aquarius', a new era, or the 'New Age' in which there would be a social revolution in the Western World. Young people led the charge against war, racism, the class system, gender inequality, homophobia, environmental devastation and the rejection of consumerist values. Music, drugs, meditation, hippies featured heavily. There was great hope that the call to 'tune in, turn on, drop out' would spark an entire societal change. Peace and free love were foreground.

The Age of Aquarius was also about a shift in consciousness, partly fuelled by the availability of psychedelic drugs such as LSD or Acid. There was interest in planetary and astrological matters, and a decline in organised religion. People were finding new ways of connecting to 'Spirit'. My friend, Pat Mary was on the scene at the time. This is how she describes it:

> I remember one sunny day in Hyde Park, dancing to 'All you need is Love'. A huge circle of us, holding hands. For me, being a teenager in the 60s was a time of freedom, experimentation, expansion of consciousness.
>
> Later I became more aware of the limitations of the sixties - 'free love' could be exploitation for many of us girls. Ageism, racism, homophobia, many other forms of oppression remained. And of course, globally, we were a privileged minority.
>
> Back then, though, I saw the hierarchical, deferential fifties give way to great waves of creativity, radical optimism, joyful celebration of life.
>
> Pat Mary Brown

I asked my parents what they were up to in the 60s. They said they were too consumed by bringing up 3 young children to be part of Swinging London. However, my mother became involved in the feminist movement in the 1970s, active in The Fawcett Society and Women in Media. She also wrote books about men and the feminist revolution and about mothers who leave their children, both somewhat revolutionary for their day.

Luckily for my sister and I, our mother modelled being a strong and independent woman, even though it was our father who brought money into the household, whilst she retained most of the domestic duties. She also encouraged us to be independent, and to look beyond the traditional roles and values that women were assigned in those times. After she died, a number of younger female family friends and relatives confirmed that she modelled something different for them too: less conventional, more creative and independent.

The 60s, as well as being of importance to my own biographical story, are also relevant to the shape of things to come in the form of the rave scene and the evolution of dance practice. The pinnacle of the 1960s counter cultural revolution was in 1967. 100,000 young people, hippies, gathered in San Francisco (and some other American cities). This became known as The First Summer of Love. It was all about living in new and different ways to the mainstream and a shift in consciousness.

1988 The Second Summer of Love

The Second Summer of Love was in 1988 - a mere 20 years later – in the UK. Acid House music had become very popular and the drug of choice for this generation was Ecstasy (or MDMA), a pleasure and empathy-inducing drug, originally designed for use in psychotherapy. Again we see the theme of young people who want to see beyond, to look wider, to reach further than the materialist world they were presented with. In the UK the Acid House scene ripped through some of the social and class barriers that had existed for many generations. It was no less revolutionary and anarchic as the First Summer of Love. It just came in a different guise.

In both cases, government crackdowns and the use of law changes brought an end to proceedings. It is said that in 1960s USA, there was real concern that the hippie movement would be so impactful that there wouldn't be enough bodies willing to fight the Vietnam War. In the UK, noise and social disturbance were the grounds for shutting down the party.

Psychedelics were outlawed in the 1960s, the hippie movement petered out in the 1970s, and yet 'The New Age' continued, unabated. The Age of Aquarius was in play. People began to get interested in Yoga, Meditation, Spirituality, Healing, Vegetarianism, Environmentalism. Young people from the West travelled to India and other parts of Asia and learnt about Buddhism, Hinduism, new ways of living and seeing the world.

Ram Dass, Social Influencer

Ram Dass, born Richard Alpert, was a big social influencer of his time and beyond. He grew up in middle class USA, became a Professor of Psychology at Harvard in the late 1950s. He worked with Timothy Leary, another Harvard professor, on the therapeutic effects of psychedelic drugs, which led to their dismissal from the university in 1963.

Having received spiritual insight from taking psychedelics, Ram Dass became interested in the phenomenology of the experience and subsequently travelled to India in search of understanding. He found his guru, Maharaji, who gave him the name Ram Dass, meaning servant of god. His role was to bring back insights from the East to a Western audience, which he did with warmth, humour and insight over the next 50 years.

Global challenges

Set against the cultural revolution of flower power and transcendental meditation, the post war decades were dominated by the cold war, the threat of nuclear war, terrorism and latterly climate change, loss of biodiversity, the threat of cyberattack, pandemics, growing understanding about the ubiquitous nature of trauma, including the impact on war of returning war vets and more.

These big challenges laid foundations for emerging generations, disillusioned with politics, organised religion, the promise of things getting better and the accumulation of money being a prerequisite for happiness. There was a desire for meaning and a way to understand the purpose of human consciousness.

Mind Body Split and Reconnection

There was something else in Western culture that was waiting to be healed. Ever since Ancient Greeks and the time of Plato, there had been an orientation towards the rational and analytic rather than knowing based on experience, the imagination, wisdom, creativity and more. It was believed that the body was primarily concerned with material existence. This theme was repeated in Christian thinking.

Later, we encounter the Cartesian Split, based on the work of Rene Descartes who is often described as the 'Father of Modern Philosophy'. The split or dualism is that mind and matter (the body) are completely separable; that they exist in different spheres. In this paradigm, rationality is espoused as optimal; the mind is our control centre through which we understand life whilst sensory information from our bodies is secondary. Any other sense of interconnectedness (soul, planetary, environmental) is unimportant.

The reconnection and rebalancing of the mind and body is the story behind the instinctual pull to dance. Our body is not an object in the world of our mind, a physical system detached from the mind. It is also an emotional system and an intelligence platform – the body is a conduit for wisdom, insight, consciousness and healing. If we can find reliable ways to work with our bodies sympathetically, our health and wisdom will improve.

> The sessions and the practice offer me a space in which I can let go, be free to express myself and take risks. I'm learning about myself in the process finding new ways to connect,.to be open and more playful. If I have had a stressful week it's really helpful to come and move, it helps me shift and process without thinking or talking.

I like the opportunity to dance with others it allows you to enter into their world; by exploring and responding to their movements and moving with them you experience that person and yourself in a way you never would in normal conversation. I like that connection with people where there's no words, it's honest.

The resting parts are as valuable as the movement; the change of pace gives me a chance to reflect within and to integrate through the music. Afterwards I can come back into the space with something different. I can feel that I know myself differently.

It is good to be part of a strong community of people that I enjoy sharing that quality of space and time with.

Ali Northcott

Anna Halprin

Anna Halprin played a big role in redefining dance in post-war USA and was part of the postmodern dance movement of the 1960s which challenged the narrow views of modern dance, claiming that all movement was dance expression and everyone was a dancer. Halprin developed a way of working that allowed people to move freely with emotion, with a sense of community and empathy for the movement of others.

She integrated therapeutic tools from the work of Fritz Perles (Gestalt Therapy), and after developing cancer herself, dedicated herself to investigating the healing potential of dance and movement, saying that to be truly healed of disease, rather than just medically cured, you had to go through another kind of process. Halprin used dance to tackle racial prejudice, another place that healing was required, forming the first multi-racial dance company in the USA. She highly valued connection with the natural world and developed the 'Planetary

Dance', a danced peace ritual practised in 46 countries around the world.

> *'Movement has the capacity to take us to the home of the soul, the world within for which we have no name. Movement reaches our deepest nature, and dance creatively expresses it. Through dance, we gain new insights into the mystery of our lives. When brought forth from the inside and forged by the desire to create personal change, dance has the profound power to heal the body, psyche and soul.'* Anna Halprin

Gabriel Roth

Gabriel Roth, founder of 5 Rhythms Dance, made the breakthrough for dancing with awareness in the body in the 1960s. She was, beyond doubt, a pioneer, the person responsible for bringing ecstasy back to dance floor in the West following centuries of mind/body estrangement. She found herself drawn to the Esalen Institute in Big Sur, California, a retreat and educational centre, and home of the Human Potential Movement (HPM).

The HPM itself was part of the 1960s counter-culture revolution offering alternative values to mainstream ideas of organised religion, lifestyle, psychology and what it means to be a fully actualised human being. It is strongly associated with Abraham Maslow's work on the Hierarchy of Needs, which suggests that once basic survival needs are met – for food, water, rest, safety and security, other psychological needs emerge: for friendship, belonging, accomplishment, culminating in the need to develop a person's full, creative potential.

Fritz Perles, the father of a new form of humanistic therapy, Gestalt Therapy, was at Esalen when Gabriel Roth arrived. He knew that she had a background in teaching movement and asked her to teach dance to his therapy groups. She reported that they were resistant to dancing, didn't know how to breathe below their heads:

> *'Sometimes two hours of moving were as powerful as two years on the couch. I discovered that the body can't lie; put it in motion and the truth kicks in... I wanted to set the breath free and release all the pent-up energies in the body that were keeping it from moving, preventing it from being inspired.'* Gabriel Roth

Through her own dance practice Roth underwent divine inspiration:

> *'God had spoken to me without saying a word...I danced till I disappeared inside the dance, till there was nothing left of me but the rhythm of my breath [in which] I felt totally connected, body and soul.'*

She realised that people had been estranged from their bodies as a form of social control. The sense of aliveness and spontaneity that comes from truly inhabiting our bodies would make people impossible to control. Her mission then was to reconnect people with a deeper, more sacred sense of self, for longed-for ecstasy, through their moving bodies.

Roth developed a movement map, the 5Rhythms: flowing, staccato, chaos, lyrical and stillness. Each rhythm had their own timbre, to guide participants through a cycle or movement process:

> *'I've found a language of patterns I can trust to deliver us into universal truths, truths older than time. In the rhythm of the body we can trace our holiness, roots that go all the way back to zero. States of being where all identities dissolve into an eternal flow of energy. Energy moves in waves. Waves move in patterns. Patterns move in rhythms. A human being is just that, energy, waves, patterns, rhythms. Nothing more. Nothing less. A dance.'*

Roth is awesome. Just reading her books, my mirror neurons fire up, and I'm back on the dancefloor. Thank you Gabrielle for giving us back to ourselves. Roth's work heralded a major opportunity to rediscover dance as a means into the consciousness of the body. No longer simply a recreational activity, a form of entertainment, dance became an activity that recruits the intelligence of the body in order to promote insight and wisdom, social bonds and belonging, and the restoration of energy flow and life force.

Contemporary Dance

Contemporary dance continued to gain popularity in the 20th century:

> '*The origins of this popular dance movement can be traced to several influential dance masters such as Isadora Duncan, Martha Graham and Merce Cunningham. They all wanted to show to the world that contemporary dancers should embrace freedom, ignore old dance conventions and explore the limits of the human body and visual expression of feelings. Also, one of the precursors to the contemporary dance can be found in the millennia's old techniques of Zen Buddhism and Indian Health Yoga, which incorporates various dancing philosophies that closely follow the principles of contemporary dance.*' [v]

Community dance

The term Community Dance emerged in the mid-70s and 80s in the USA following the ideological shifts prompted by the Civil Rights, Peace, Environmental, and Women's Liberation Movements. Conventions of every sort were being challenged, including those around race, class and gender. Since that time, Community Dance has orientated itself to being *of* the people and *for* the people and has embraced dance as a catalyst for change.

Community dance transcends differences of culture, age, disability, race, religion, gender and sexual orientation. By dancing together we create community; a space, a place where everyone can feel included, and can in turn move and include their own feelings, thoughts and physical sensations, responding to the music and each other with our bodies.

Community Dance is not about any specific type of dance but is more concerned with engaging people to be creative and connect with others through their moving body. It can involve performance, talking, watching and learning about dance. Participants do not need to want to work in the field of dance or perform to a set standard.

Typically, Community Dance is aimed at minority and vulnerable groups in society to provide opportunities that would not otherwise be available, for example in under-privileged ethnic groups and older people with dementia. The benefits to wellbeing are plentiful and well researched. In every case, it is as much about finding expression for a community as creating a community through dance.

Polyvagel Theory

In recent decades, the medical and science world have made big discoveries that support embodied practices, especially in the sphere of neuroscience. Polyvagal Theory, sometimes called the Science of Safety was introduced by Steven Porges in 1994. It showed that there were bi-directional pathways between body and brain; that psychological processes impact body states, and importantly that what goes on in the body colours perception.

> *'New ways of thinking have emerged that place the body, movement and dance in a much more central place than what they had previously, and with renewed significance for wellbeing.'*
> The Oxford Handbook of Dance and Wellbeing.

Polyvagal Theory offers a modern map of the autonomic nervous system (ANS) and the way it reacts to experiences and regulates responses. There are two primary experiences that exist in the autonomic nervous system: the biological need to connect and the wired-in drive to protect and survive. Porges introduced the idea of 'neuroception' which describes how the ANS interfaces with the world. It works below the level of awareness and responds to cues of safety or danger in the environment, inside the body or in relationships with people.

The ANS has evolved over time with human evolution. The oldest part is the parasympathetic dorsal vagal state which uses immobilization to survive. Then came the sympathetic nervous system which added mobilization strategies of fight or flight. And finally and most recently the parasympathetic ventral vagal state offers safety through connection and social engagement.

Vagus, meaning wanderer in Latin, is the main component of the ANS, and is divided into two parts (hence wanderer): dorsal and ventral vagal. It originates in the brainstem and connects to most of our organs, wandering up into our head and face, and down as far as our intestinal tract. Importantly the pathways are bi-directional and in fact 80% of information comes from the body to the brain.

The sympathetic nervous system originates in the spinal cord and works with the ventral vagal system to bring energy to life's activities. When triggered into survival response, the sympathetic nervous system pumps the hormones adrenalin and cortisol throughout the body for fight or flight.

Deb Dana, clinician and consultant specializing in helping people with trauma, wrote in her book Polyvagal Exercises for Safety and Connection:

> *'Your clients' stories begin in their bodies. Science has shown that behind the scenes, the autonomic nervous system, through habitual patterns of response, generates stories. With awareness and practice, you can help your clients reshape their responses and rewrite their stories.'*

Conscious Movement and Polyvagel Theory

Enter conscious dance. There are various ways in which conscious dance supports healthy ANS function. Firstly, the invitation to consciously inhabit our bodies, in any way we choose, in the safe guidance of a facilitator, communicates a direct experience of safety and connection. With brain and body being in constant state of change, greater awareness in our bodies also can bring insight to when misattunement, or danger, is sensed. With awareness comes choice to find connection with others, or self, and to return to ventral vagal safety. Movement and dance are themselves ways of moving out of nervous system dysregulation back to regulation.

> *'The ability to turn toward and fully experience body sensations as you move is therapeutic. Movement practices are a form of autonomic exercise that shapes the system. Both the actual physical act of moving and bringing movement to life in your imagination activate the autonomic nervous system.'* Dana

Dance generally involves interaction and communication with others. Aside from the muscular bonding, identified by O'Neill, it is the social engagement of dance that allows people to regulate their ANS and establish connection with others. Conscious movement repeatedly brings our attention to breath, much like meditation, and adds further regulating benefits.

> *'Breathing, thinking and feeling are tied together through the autonomic nervous system (MA et al 2017), and simple breath practices synchronize heart and breath activity which is a function of the vagal pathways leading to 'a positive effect on physical, emotional and relational wellbeing.'* Dana

A key message from Polyvagal Theory is that the stories we tell ourselves, - indeed the very way we see the world - is located in the body, deep within our nervous system with its concern of safety and survival. In the light of this, engaging with conscious dance makes sense in terms of its regulating, relational and biophysical qualities.

Conscious Dance v Self-Conscious Dance

Conscious dance or movement is about embodied awareness. We bring attention to the sensations and feelings in our body; we notice thoughts and feelings and find ways of expressing these through movement without having to find words or provide explanations.

As we go about our lives, we develop habits and patterns of thinking and engaging with the world through the conscious thoughts we are having and through early survival patterns which are often outside of awareness. Conscious movement frees this up; we have other dimensions and resources to draw upon for the way we live and relate. This is deeply liberating and creative.

When we are 'self' conscious, we are preoccupied with how others see us. In therapy terms, we talk about putting our own thoughts and feelings onto other people as 'projection'; it is considered a defence mechanism to avoid uncomfortable feelings.. It is also an 'outside in' way of being. Our attention is not rooted in our own sensory grounded experience, it is outside of ourselves imagining what others are thinking and feeling about us.

When we are conscious, we are more in touch with what we are experiencing; in movement this means we are more connected to what is going on in our bodies and our breath, moment to moment. It is an 'inside out' way of being, attuned to sensations, feelings and thoughts that are arising within us.

The more we practice conscious movement, anchored in awareness of our own bodies and processes, the more we loosen our focus on what others are thinking about us (self-consciousness). The dance takes over and becomes the predominating experience; paradoxically our sense of being a separate 'self' dissolves. We are no longer 'making' the dance happen, the experience is one of 'being danced'. This is the gift of freedom.

Trauma and the body

In 2014 a book was published that helped put trauma and the body centre stage. It is The Body Keeps the Score by psychiatrist and neuroscientist, Dr Bessel Van Der Kolk. It has since become a New York Times number 1 bestseller. The book explains that trauma is the result of an experience or event that was too overwhelming for a person to deal with.

Instead of moving on from the experience, the sufferer keeps behaving like they are in danger and the symptoms of this show up in the body: they can become frozen and still, or hypervigilant to their surroundings. The body keeps the score in the sense that the body is like a scoresheet of the emotional experiences that the person has been through.

Van Der Kolk's answer is:

> *'To have experiences that deeply and viscerally contradict the helplessness, rage or collapse that resulted from trauma.' He says that mainstream psychiatry only uses drugs and verbal therapies to change the way we feel and pay little attention to 'self-management' as oppose to: 'other traditions from around the world [that] rely on mindfulness, movement, rhythms, and action.'* Van Der Kolk.

He says that neuroscience research shows that the only way to change the way we feel is by paying attention and befriending our inner experiences. *'This means that we can directly train our arousal system by the way we breathe, chant, and move, a principle that has been utilized since time immemorial in places like China and India, and in every religious practice...but that is suspiciously eyed as "alternative" in mainstream [Western} culture'.* Van Der Kolk.

We can see here that conscious dance which is all about dancing with awareness of the body and attention to breath, is a helpful tool for unifying mind and body and bypassing the alarm signal that trauma creates.

In her excellent work on integrating trauma, Elizabeth Dennison talks about:

> *'building the capacity to tolerate what was overwhelming and intolerable in the past, so our nervous system can digest and metabolize fragments of experience that we have split off or numbed down.'* vi

She says that:

> *'We can...expand our physical awareness so more parts carry the same embodied charge. Resourcing, titrating and discharging are essential tools in this process. Resourcing keeps us hopeful and connected with pleasant or tolerable experiences. Titrating prevents re-traumatisation, and allows us to work more efficiently and precisely. Discharge can clear the excess charge as we reconnect with intense experiences. Discharge can also expand our capacity to sit with the charge of physically intense experience so we can integrate it.'*

Conscious dance can be a helpful space to practice being more present in our bodies. In doing this we can begin to develop the skills and resources to support us when life feels overwhelming and challenging.

Dance for Life

" I used to love Dance as a child. Who doesn't? Dance is a natural expression which has as adults becomes loaded over time with judgement, self-consciousness and 'getting it right'. I went to drama school where dance was part of the daily routine, instructions shouted by teachers who were moulding future ballerinas. It was stressful and I was not one of the best.

I left drama school, relieved. I no longer had dance. There was no pleasure in it for me, full of judgements rules and regulations no longer allowing free expression that I had loved as a child! Dance was also for me, was associated with an obsession around weight, and how you looked, as the teachers used to weigh us every week. I left with no love of Dance, high levels of anxiety, physical pain, and huge amount of effort to be driven in my daily activities. In other words, stress.

After years of discomfort in body and mind, I discovered the Alexander Technique, which is a profound and powerful method that enabled me to discover inner freedom and effortless poise. I have been practicing this ever since and was overjoyed to have discovered Flomotion. For me, the two are perfect and in harmony with each other. Flomotion has reconnected me with the inner freedom and spontaneous dance I used to enjoy naturally as a child. This class embodies freedom of expression and lack of judgement. To move to beautiful music, without the strict instructions of conventional dance classes is essential for my inner being and health. Flomotion is incredibly therapeutic, non-judgemental and enjoyable.

I actually attended the class by accident as my best friend invited me to this which I thought was a show. I was horrified I realised it was actually a class I needed to participate in. It was huge surprise when I found self-consciousness falling away, and I was able to dance freely and loved it! I was addicted from then and I'm a dedicated member of the class. It is an incredibly supportive environment which I look forward to fortnightly. I'm very grateful that Flomotion has created this space for all of us to come together in silence and freedom to move as we wish.

Delphine Miller

Health and Dance

Understanding about the impact of stress, trauma and the demands of an increasingly complex, sedentary lifestyles, have piqued interest in fitness activities, including dance. There have been many studies which again and again show how beneficial dancing is. In their book, Dancing is the Best Medicine, Julia F. Christensen and Dong-Seon Chang, site many research papers that tell us:

> *'Dancing trains our motor skills, self-perception, and memory, and it enhances our freedom, our creativity, our emotions, and our community. It strengthens our cardiovascular system and our immune system, improves our posture, and keeps us nimble and flexible into old age. Dancing improves our mood and confidence and, coincidentally, provides a great workout that makes us lose weight and tighten up. Finally, and most important, dancing goes straight to the brain and strengthens connections between nerve cells: we learn more easily and keep mentally fit. What other movement can do all that? Dance is a miracle drug.'*

Zumba, Salsa, Capoeira, Mambo and Tango.

Zumba arrived as a dance and fitness craze in the 1990s from a Columbian dancer Beto Perez. It is a style of aerobics with Latin rhythms, whose invitation is to 'ditch the workout, join the party'. It is hugely popular with more than 15 million people taking classes weekly all over the globe.

Other Latin-inspired dance including Salsa, which originated in Cuba at the turn of the 20th century. It is said to be one of the most practised social dances in the world today. Other popular Latin dances are: Bachata, Merengue, Cha Cha Cha, Rumba, Samba, Mambo and Tango.

Capoeira combines martial art, dance, and spirituality. It is an ever-evolving Afro-Brazilian art form that began in the 18th century within the enslaved African community. It takes place in a human circle where people play rhythmic music and sing, and participants take turns to perform acrobatic and complex movement. In 2014 it was protected by UNESCO as an intangible cultural heritage.

Dance organisations

International Dance Day was created in 1982 to celebrate dance on a global scale. It takes place each year on 29 April, the anniversary of the birth of the 'father' of modern ballet, Jean-George Noverre (1727-1810):

> *'This day is a celebration day for those who can see the value and importance of the art form "dance", and acts as a wake-up-call for governments, politicians and institutions which have not yet recognised its value to the people and to the individual and have not yet realised its potential for economic growth.'*
> International Theatre Institute – world organization for the performing arts, partnered with UNESCO. vii

Dance medicine and science emerged from sports medicine as a field of study in the 1970s and 1980s. In 1990 the International Association for Dance, Medicine and Science (IADMS) was formed. It's a global network medical professionals, dancers, researchers and educators. Here's their mission:

> '*IADMS is an inclusive organization for professionals who care for those who dance by evolving best practices in dance science, education, research, and medical care to support optimal health, well-being, training, and performance.*' viii

There are at least 17 national dance organisations in the UK ranging from the Association of Dance of the African Diaspora (ADAD) to the Royal Academy of Dance (RAD), and around 10 International dance organisations. There's even a Dance World Cup with 62 countries and 120,000 competitors participating from all over the world.

Diary of a Conscious Dance Teacher, Thursday

Tired today. I can feel fatigue in my ribs, breath is shallow. The rain is coming down with no let-up expected. I worry that the numbers will be low on Saturday as people opt for sofa over dancefloor. Don't blame them.

A whole heap of grief came pouring down on me today. It was like a heavy tornado came in really fast. I was overcome and overwhelmed. My back was full of pain, and I felt sick to the core. Deep breath was not easy to access. I put some music on, slow, classical dance. I started to move; brain busy with 'this is not going to help' 'stop that' 'do something' 'no energy for that'.

Soon enough the magic happened. The music and movement became more compelling than the riot of fear cursing through my body with its playmates: story upon story of my demise and disaster. At some point I stopped 'trying' to dance, and something moved through me. Tears, big feelings, more tears, AND something precious and beautiful and poignant was happening. Something bigger than me and my story.

I am able to embrace more; there's more of life (of me?) available. I am tender and grateful.

BBC Just One Thing - Dance

Interest in health and wellbeing have surged in recent decades and dance is on the agenda. Dr Michael Mosley in his BBC Radio 4 series, Just One Thing, investigated a number of activities that are scientifically proven to change your life and there dancing excelled. He saw evidence to show that dance improves memory, boosts immune system, enhances heart and brain health, improves mood, supports good posture and flexibility, aids sleep, decreases stress, reduces hypertension and increases our ability to be empathic towards others. Latest research also reveals that dancing can be as effective as high intensity interval training. What's not to like?

Here's some of the research sited by Dr Mosley:

- A study of 50,000 adults over 12 years showed that dancing, compared to 'other activities', was linked to a reduced risk of stroke or heart attack.
- A Korean study trialled dance as a way of treating depressed adolescents. After 12 weeks, there were significant improvements in self-reported scores for psychological distress and raised levels of serotonin, a mood-stabilizing hormone.
- A study of older adults revealed that frequent dancing was associated with 76% reduced risk of developing dementia.

Dr Mosley explains that brain imaging studies show that dancing increases the volume of the hippocampus, the part of the brain that deals with spatial memory. Dance increases this volume more than traditional fitness exercises. Dance has also been shown to improve 'white matter', the number of nerve cells in areas of the brain associated with processing speed and memory. Again, this was not seen in groups doing other forms of exercise.

Dr Mosley concludes that: *'Dancing is a good workout for pretty much every system in the body'*. He says that including dance in your routine for only 10 minutes a day, really could benefit your body and your life. ix

In this chapter we have looked at the revival of dance in the West, the emergence of conscious movement, understandings about the autonomous nervous system, trauma, the popularity of dance and some current research that demonstrate the significant health benefits of dance.

> I discovered dancing in school and church hall style discos in my early teen. I lived in a hamlet in West Wales. I loved the freedom of movement, the loud music and the escape from everyday life.
>
> I had children in my 30s and life became a bit more sedate. I tried returning to clubs but found them too loud and too late for early parenting to be compatible. In my 40s I was reduced to dancing around my kitchen alone and the occasional long night at a party, if I could persuade the host to turn down the lights and crank up the sound system.
>
> Last year I was introduced to Flomotion. I was reluctant at first to go along, not knowing what to expect. What I found on my first night was joy and freedom. Over the weeks becoming more mindful of what I was experiencing and what I had been missing: the energy of good

music; the connection to others on the dance floor; and the escape from day to day stresses.

Over the past 12 months my experience of this type of dance practice has not only fed my need to move but has begun to stretch my understanding of how you can work through mental issues by allowing music to challenge different movement. Most importantly, I have found a new community around dance where I can be playful and less serious.

EL

> I am a dancer and dancing in community has become a new practice. Each time is unique with a common thread of leaving the dancefloor feeling joyful, content and grounded.
>
> Dancing in community is sharing my experience. The act of giving generously to others the expression of my movement and the history that goes along with it.
>
> And afterwards, to voice my inner experience with words that embody the emotions. I feel seen and heard in a common language. that is often not accessible in other friendship circles.

JP

FOUR

The Place of Dance in today's world

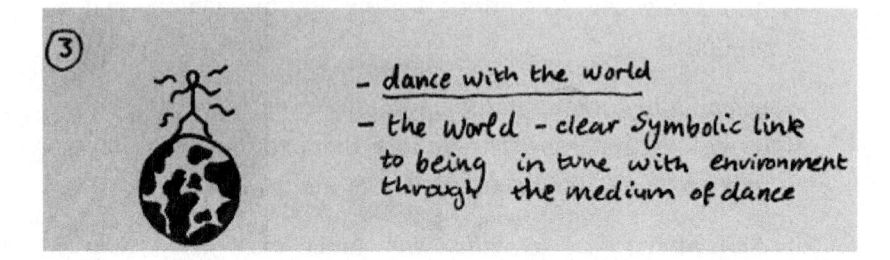

> ③
> — dance with the world
> — the World - clear Symbolic link to being in tune with environment through the medium of dance

As we have seen, there is a massive interest in dance throughout the world these days. TikTok is full of it; people watch Strictly avidly on TV in the UK and the format has been exported to 60 other countries, the online space is full of dance, books and articles are being written about the benefits of dance from doctors, psychologists, dance leaders, neuroscientists, music experts and more. Ecstatic dance has captured the imagination of a generation of ex-ravers looking for the highs and connection on the dancefloor.

The many benefits of dance

In this chapter, we focus on areas where dance is making a substantial impact in the quality of people's lives, backed up by significant evidence and research. This supports a proposition that we no longer think of dance as a marginal, recreational activity, rather one that can be transformative at a personal and collective level, can provide healing and real benefits to people's health and wellbeing and may even hold an important opportunity for social change.

Gill Clarke, MBE, wrote about the important contribution that dancers could make as 'harbourers of an embodied knowledge'. She was described by The Guardian as 'one of the foremost contemporary dancers of her generation…She had the capacity to immerse herself in movement until her presence seemed to merge into a bigger idea: the dance itself.' Here's what she said:

> *'As we have evolved as humans our ever more sophisticated, analytical brains have been taking over control. Instead of turning our developed intelligence inward to better understand how we live through our bodies, or outwards to understand our symbiotic relationship with the natural world, our intelligence seems paradoxically to be directing us towards an existence beyond the body, with need only of a brain in order to operate and design technology. A rational and technological arrogance has gradually led us away from 'relationship', and towards an ecological tipping point - in terms of the sustainability of our external environment and our bodily health.'* x

In her recent fascinating book, Dance Your Way Home, Emma Warren, boldly says:

> *'Perhaps dancing together, informally and without too many rules, can also suggest a route through the combined messes of late-stage capitalism, climate change, racism and new nationalism – even if it's simply a replenishment.'*

> *'I believe that moving to music is an effective way to see ourselves and each other, and to re-synchronise and rebuild,*

regardless of what has been demolished – hopes and dreams, an economy, the future…The more we improvise movement, together, the better the chance of we have of thickening our relationships, building the necessary connections we need for a future that looks increasingly low-resource and local.'

'What if dance could save the world?' was the title of a recent article in the New York Times which tracked how dance had been showing its 'broader worth' in many contexts from music videos, stage, film, movement classes and TikTok tutorials. *It goes on:*

'Our lives are full of words…Dance can say what words often can't. It can be watched, it can be felt through the watching, and it can be a physical part of anyone's life…Dance gives us the ability to see beyond the obvious.'

'At this moment when dance is everywhere, it's time to give it deeper attention... Dance isn't separate from life; movement is a part of life, after all…Maybe dance can save the world. Maybe it's not maybe. Maybe, under the radar, dance has already been changing the world in unassuming ways…where movement is seen and shared through the bodies and minds of everyday dancers.' xi

Elizabeth Dennison, author and found of The Center for Body-Up Regulation, makes this claim about body awareness:

'When we are in the habit of ignoring our body awareness and our bodily needs, it seems normal to ignore environmental degradation and (inconvenient) awareness of others and their needs.' vi

So how is dancing so good for us?

Where to start. Dance has proven benefits to our cardiovascular system, immune system, posture, weight control, hormonal balance, endurance, stamina, motor skills, memory, improved learning ability and more.

> *'Dancing has the added benefit of using almost every muscle in the body',*

we are told by two neuroscientists, Christensen and Chang.

> I have noticed an opening and growing confidence in clients who are part of Flomotion and other conscious dance practices. The ability to drop into the body through dance and movement allows emotional blockages to come to the surface…to be felt and released, in a safe and held space, resulting in layers being shed, deeper connection to self and embodied healing.
>
> Deborah Laniado

Healthy Living Agenda

In recent years, The University of Exeter and Trinity Laban Conservatoire have been involved in a number of research projects to:

> *'consider[ed] the distinctive aesthetic, artistic and creative contributions that dance can make to health and wellbeing and [what are] the range of methodologies that can capture them best.'* xii

This research indicates that dance has the capacity to play a 'vital' part in the healthy-living agenda. As a non-competitive form of exercise it contributes significantly to mental and physical health in different populations in the community.

Stress

Let's talk about dance and stress for a minute. Beyond doubt humans have always had to face adversity and have found ways to cope. On a physiological level, when we are stressed, we produced stress hormones: adrenalin, cortisol, insulin and noradrenalin, which in evolutionary terms was a way to escape from danger, or fight the danger. Once these actions have been implemented, the whole organism can recalibrate. Another response is to 'play dead' or freeze.

The stressors of modern life: mobiles, electronic devices, demanding jobs, failing economies, planetary breakdown etc do not necessarily neutralise our heightened vigilance, and the hormones created by the stress have nowhere to go. In the long run, if this isn't released we become burnt out, ill, and exhausted. Many people use sport, the gym and other aerobic activity to clear the cortisol in their system. Scientific research backs this up.

Dance, it turns out, is another highly effective way. In her book, Dancing for Health: Conquering and Preventing Stress, Judith Lynne Hanna (dance educator and anthropologist) demonstrates the many ways that dance is a healing art for all kinds of stress. She takes a wide view, looking at historic, Western and Non-Western approaches to stress and dance, showing that many cultures have used dance to face the human challenges of conflicts, life crisis and a 'litany of stressors' from natural disasters to disease, terrorism, war and ultimately death. She says that loss of control is central to an individual's stress experience:

> *'Since early history and across cultures, humans have turned to dance, a full expression of mind and body and self, as a talisman against stress'.* Hanna

Importantly Hanna backs up the idea that stress is normal, but it is the persistence and a person's inability to normalise and release stress that create chronic and acute health problems:

> *'Pathology lies not in the symptoms – a normal reaction to stress – but in the persistence of the symptoms and the amount of distress they cause.'*

She also acknowledges that dance itself can be a stressor in terms of those in performative roles having to conform to certain body images and shapes.

Isolation

It is now widely recognised that dance is a very effective way to combat social isolation, especially since the Covid pandemic. There is a myriad of research papers that look into this social phenomenon, and they consistently report that dance is a very good way to help people feel less alone and more connected with others, even when this is done via an online platform.

In the preface to her poetry book, Hard Times Require Furious Dancing, Alice Walker speaks of her own life challenges and having been *'a person of periodic deep depressions'*. This along with the collective challenges of our time: war, greed, poverty and climate emergency lead her to the dancefloor: *'I didn't know how basic it is for maintaining balance'*. She concludes:

> *'Hard Times require furious dancing. Each of us is the proof'.*

Here's what a National Geographic article says about the global rise in popularity of dance following the Covid lockdowns:

> *'...dance has been... the solution for hundreds of thousands of*

people around the world, lifting our spirits and connecting us with every single step'.

'Creative dancers share genes with strong social communicators, suggesting that we evolved to overcome social isolation'.

The article goes on to talk about International World Dance Day:' This annual UNESCO-supported event celebrates dance and encourages governments to recognise its social and educational significance'. The article quotes Gregory Vuyani Maqoma, an acclaimed South African dancer and educator who wrote the 2020 International World Dance Day message:

'More than ever, we need to dance with purpose to remind the world that humanity still exists…Our purpose is one that strives to change the world one step at a time.' xiii

Diary of conscious dance teacher, Friday

During lockdown, we danced every week at the online session Friday Flomotion. I would wake up, charge up my mini-microphones and write a meditation for the end of each session. I was doing Julia Cameron's morning pages at the time (a free-association writing exercise each morning). Here's an excerpt …

'29 of us on the Zoom dance last night. People are saying how much the weekly sessions mean to them at this time of lockdown and isolation. One person said "it's the thing that keeps us all going at this time"; someone else said it was the highlight of her week. I feel a strong sense of commitment and of purpose in bringing people together in these days of separation and loneliness.'

Today I am feeling quite flat. My father died 6 months ago, and now my mother-in-law is in her last days. My memo-

ries of them are so vivid: only a couple of years ago, Sunday night was like an old-time music hall round our house: Vera Lynn, Gene Kelly, Frank Sinatra ... endless rounds of Nelly Dean. We danced and sang together. These were always the most fun parts of the evening.

Again I wonder about music and dance; it doesn't solve real world medical, scientific or technological problems. It won't fix the climate emergency or end poverty, war and inequality. And it delivers us something so important; it's staring us in the face, and yet can so easily be side-lined and forgotten.

Heartened by this thought, I return to this week's playlist. Too many tracks with the same beat; I've over-flavoured the jazz feel. Time to tweak.

And while we're on the benefits of dance, just a couple more things…

Fitness

In their book, Dancing is the Best Medicine, neuroscientists Christensen and Chang cite numerous studies showing how beneficial dance is for our cardiovascular system. They tell us:

> 'If we dance regularly, our health benefits more than from regular participation in any other sport. Why might that be? According to the Australian research team, it's because dance not only revs up our muscles and cardiovascular system but also has important effects on our brain; these, in turn, have a positive effect on our hormonal balance.'

Chang and Christensen also make the point that we often don't notice how quickly time flies, and this means that we keep going for longer than we would in other exercise. They conclude that with its myriad benefits to many systems of the human body, dance should be available on prescription. Interestingly below, we will see that dance has been prescribed for social benefits as well as mental and physical health.

I asked some participants at Flomotion, who wear fitness or activity trackers to log their steps and calorie count during a 2 hour flomotion dance session. The results were impressive: the dancers covered an average of 11,000 steps during the session and between 300 and 400 calories were burnt. And all whilst having fun, releasing stress and feeling connected to other people.

Social prescribing

In 2019, the World Health Organisation Regional Office for Europe produced its first report looking at evidence that arts activities can promote health. This included the use of dance and music in health promotion and the prevention of ill health including amongst marginalised groups. The results were very positive, concluding that:

> *'...specific arts activities, provide additional options to traditional biomedical treatments, and should be more widely considered. Increased investment in research evaluating arts for health could generate promising returns.'*

Social prescribing is a UK NHS funded activity that 'connects people to activities, groups, and services in their community to meet the practical, social and emotional needs that affect their health and wellbeing... Social prescribing is an all-age, whole population approach that works particularly well for people who... need support with low level mental health issues [and]...who are lonely or isolated...'

The NHS programme states:

> *'This is the biggest investment in social prescribing by any national health system and legitimises non-medical community-*

based activities and holistic support alongside medical treatment as part of a personalised care approach.' xiv

Can you imagine, next time you go to the GP you might walk away with a ticket to dance? Here's one such project…

The World, 'public radio's longest-running daily global news program' ran a feature in 2022 called Dancing Away the Loneliness about social prescriptions in the UK and how these are used to combat loneliness and isolation. Here's what they said:

'Doctors now know that social isolation is linked to an increased risk of health problems like dementia, heart disease and stroke. Loneliness also increases the risk of high blood pressure. And people with fewer connections are also at greater risk of premature death. In 2017, US Surgeon General Vivek Murthy called loneliness an epidemic.'

The UK, Japan and Australia have all developed national strategies for loneliness. The World feature focused on a project in Hackney, London, called the Posh Club, a weekly afternoon tea club and cabaret strictly for the over 60s. People experiencing isolation and loneliness can be referred there by their GP. As well as entertainment in the form of comedy, drag performance, music and dance, attendees are also encouraged to participate in dance. Needless to say it's a vibrant and life-changing community.

> While reading an early draft of this book, I had a sudden, vivid memory of my parents doing Scottish dancing in their later years, way back in the 80s. I remember my Dad mentioning a fellow dancer, Michael Argyle, an eminent Oxford psychologist. He was writing a book about happiness and told my Dad that research showed that dancing contributes to happiness. It certainly brought my parents great joy.

Reading on, I then felt inspired to have a dance myself! I was unwell, so decided to dance for just 5 minutes. I put on a favourite, uplifting piece of music, managed to stop thinking, and as I danced, felt as if I was shaking out something that was affecting my energy levels. It came to me that a recent event had probably triggered childhood trauma. Perhaps that had knocked my immune system a bit, who knows. I'm a complete novice dancer, it hasn't really been my thing, but I thought, maybe I'll start dancing again.

Pat Mary Brown

Ageing

Phil Hilton recently wrote a piece in the UK newspaper, *The Guardian*:

I'm an older man and I love to dance. What's wrong with that?

Nothing, I say, absolutely nothing! He says:

'Beneath my disguise as a midlife professional, parent and husband, I am a clubber, I have always been a clubber. I just learned to keep it a secret.' xv

In his article, Phil sites a study published in the New England Journal of Medicine which says that 'dancing is an extraordinarily healthy activity for mature people', and importantly that **dance was the best physical activity for reducing the risk of dementia.** The piece clearly hit a nerve: he received nearly 400 comments on the first day of publishing.

Conscious Dance is MADE for older people. No booze, no drugs, daytime and early evening events, friendly and inclusive crowd, permission to follow the energy levels of your own body. In moments it can feel like you're in a nightclub, and then there's time to recoup and relax to mellow music. It's a chance to have some fun!

For other older folk who want to re-live their nightclub experiences *with* alcohol available but still have the chance of getting to bed by 10pm, London is hosting 'Day Fever', an afternoon nightclub experience, hugely popular with the older age group. Here's a couple of punters:

> *'I've always missed going clubbing…I wondered why clubs weren't doing stuff for older people because there's no reason why we would stop wanting to go out. Places are making a mistake not targeting the grey pound.'*

> *'I'm in my 50s, we're the generation who invented rave in Ibiza. We were London ravers, too cool for school. It makes sense to us.'* xvi

Dance Movement Psychotherapy

Dance Movement Therapy (DMP) emerged as a discipline in the twenty years between 1950 and 1970, and only began producing training courses in the 1980s and 90s. The field has attracted widespread interest following evidenced-based research showing significant results and is practised in a wide range of settings and with diverse groups: people with dementia, PTSD, Parkinson's Disease, birth preparation and more.

Here's how the British Association of Dance Movement Psychotherapists defines DMP:

> *'Dance Movement Psychotherapy (DMP) is a relational process in which client(s) and therapist use body movement and dance as an instrument of communication during the therapy process.'* xvii

Dance movement therapy (DMP) might take place on a one-to-one basis or in a group. It often starts with a warm-up and/or verbal check in. The therapist and client(s) might decide on a theme for the session, or there may be a programme to follow designed by the therapist. In the session itself, the therapist will guide the client into movement/dance that reflects the client's emotional state, either by free associating or representing an internal challenge. The therapist might mirror the client's movement, watch or dance with them. Special attention is paid to certain body movements or breath to sharpen awareness and focus. At the end the therapist and client(s) will discuss and integrate the session.

Parkinson's Disease

Dancing has proved to be especially helpful to people with Parkinsons's Disease, a degenerative illness that affects mobility, mood, thinking and more. This has attracted widespread international research and the results have been immensely favourable both for the physical challenges of the illness, but also for the mental and emotional side. The reason dance is so beneficial to this condition is that it demands a lot from the brain all at one time: visual, auditory, tactile, kinaesthetic as well as relational and social aspects are all at play. Other exercise does not cover this range.

Here's Dr Peter Lovatt - who himself conducted research into dance and Parkinson's - from his book, The Dance Cure:

> *'Dancing, like thinking, allows us to flex muscles that transcend a purely physical realm – it affects our social, cognitive and emotional health and means that, when we dance, we give a boost to all these aspects of our lives.'*

Dr Lovatt's research shows that improvised dance is especially helpful with being creative and innovative in many aspects of professional life. Even, taking up different postures turns out to change the way we act and feel, and even walking in different directions supports more creativity and imaginative thinking. He says, 'If you want to make changes in the way you think, then start with the way you move'.

Dementia

Dementia affects 50 million people globally and is expected rise to 115.4 million by 2050. We have seen that dance is beneficial for people with dementia, and ongoing research continues to show that it improves cognitive, physical, emotional and social performance. Studies also show that dance is effective at preventing dementia (see Michael Mosely above).

The science on dancing and dementia is clear and there is plenty of it. One such piece published in the British Medical Journal (2019) found that regular dancing led to a 20-30% lower risk of dementia and depression, a 20-35% lower risk of cardiovascular disease, a 20% lower risk of breast cancer and a 30% lower risk of colon cancer.

There are many projects and services now running dance groups for people who have dementia. For example, Scottish Ballet runs sessions for people living with dementia, their family and carers. They say:

> *'By developing communication, expression, coordination, balance, creativity, problem-solving and social interaction, dancing supports brain health and improves quality of life.'*
> Xviii

The Dance Network is a dance charity that 'enables people to live more connected, joyful and aspirational lives through dance'. They provide opportunities for people to improve their confidence and physical well-being, whilst encouraging creativity, independent thinking and friendship through social interaction. Amongst other things they offer dance sessions for people with dementia, those with Parkinson's and dance for older adults. xviii

Dance and Children

There is plenty of research that shows that Dance Movement Therapy with children builds their sense of worth, empowers them to overcome obstacles and helps regulate emotions and reactions. Work with children and young people who have been resettled as refugees shows that it reduces symptoms of PTSD and anxiety and helps to build resilience.

In 2019 it was reported that nearly a third of children aged 2 to 15 are overweight or obese with the associated risks to physical and mental health. Ofsted (the UK national body that monitors educational standards, children's services and skills) identified that dance should be a key tool for tackling obesity in primary school children especially for those less interested in organised sport. Interestingly, dance is now the second most commonly offered physical activity in UK schools' physical education curriculum after football. Dance is also being used in other ways in education: for example to teach maths and chemistry. In educational theory, it increasingly understood that children who dance regularly have better learning skills and neural flexibility, as well as serving as a mood stabilizer.

Eating Disorders

Dance movement therapy (DMT) is used successfully around the world for people with eating disorders to find new ways to relate to their bodies. By helping people to become aware of body sensations and feelings, the therapy can help people listen to their body's needs instead of the tendency to avoid feelings, focus on body distortions, obsessive and binary thinking. DMT provides a structure in which clients can safely be in their bodies, express themselves through their movement, get closer to feelings and see patterns that underly their behaviour.

Anxiety and Depression

Dance Movement Therapy is widely used for the treatment of anxiety and depression. Sometimes clients need ways of expressing emotion and relating other than by simply having a verbal conversation. DMT adds an additional channel for expression. Depression, anxiety and trauma can also result in people disconnecting from their bodies or disassociating. Movement is a great antidote to this.

Dance is also very beneficial to mental health because it allows us relief from day-to-day concerns and interrupts negative looping thoughts. It also has the benefit of being a group activity strongly associated with bonding, community- building and is a great antidote to social isolation.

Research based on a survey of 1,000 people across the world practising conscious dance 'produced mental health benefits among the vast majority of participants with depression, anxiety or history of trauma.' The research was carried out by the University of California, Los Angeles, in August 2021. 81% of people in the survey self-reported chronic pain, stress-related health conditions, history of addiction/substance abuse, trauma, depression or anxiety. Some of the participants were in the 70s and 80s, again showing how beneficial these practices are to people of all ages.

In the research 98% of participants said the dancing improved their mood, with large numbers reporting 'therapeutic benefits', greater confidence and enhanced compassion. They also described feeling more present in their bodies, more relaxed, more present in the moment, more aware of their emotions and having a greater sense of meaning and purpose.

The senior author of the study, Dr Prabha Siddarth, offered this understanding of the results:

> *'The spontaneity, inward focus and sensory awareness of the movement...allows participants to go into what they call "being*

in the zone" or "in the flow". When one does that, you sort of let go of your prefrontal activity…you allow your emotional brain to take over. That's at least the hypothesis of why it has these beneficial psychological, well-being effects.' Siddarth xix

Addiction

Dance Movement Therapy has been used for decades as a way of treating addictions. It allows people to put into motion complex thoughts and feelings that might otherwise be hard to express, including trauma, and offers a pathway to processing these difficulties. It offers bodily freedom, empowerment and enables creative responses.

In addition to the Dance Movement Therapy route, some addiction recovery programmes offer creative movement classes that draw on several traditions to tackle stress, express emotions, increase self-esteem and connect with self, others and community.

An example is The Fallen Angel Dance Company. It is unique in the UK for offering dance experiences to people recovering from addiction. It was set up in 2011 by a recovering alcoholic dancer, Paul Bayes Kitcher and Clare Morris. Their 'methods link creative dance practice to recognisable processes in addiction rehabilitation', using breathwork and visualisation to awaken the body and quiet the mind.

Their sessions include standard features of support groups, including check-ins and check-outs, alongside core elements of ballet and contemporary dance such as sequences and improvisation techniques. The themes that they explore include feeling safe with others, finding solidarity, reaching beyond challenges and trauma, exploring freedom and choice.

One Fallen Angel Company member recently described her experience:

> '…there is true, true love and joy in everything we do. I've found a family within Fallen Angels'. xx

In this chapter we have discovered the many ways in which dance is being used all around the world today to tackle a myriad of mental, emotional and physical health issues, aimed at young and older people, the able-bodied and those with disabilities.

In the next chapter we will focus specifically on conscious dance, the various types and what you might expect from attending a conscious dance session.

> As a child I loved ballet, the feeling of putting my body into motion, especially where I had space to improvise my own dance. I experienced significant trauma in my teenage years and coped by disowning aspects of myself. This included deciding that I would no longer dance. I became the adult who everyone knew didn't dance.
>
> As I found ways to truly heal from my past trauma, I became aware of a growing need in me to dance. I heard about conscious dance but was struggling to find the courage to attend a physical class. One of the few good things to come from the Covid-19 lockdown for me was that dancing moved online. Dancing in this way, in the safety of my own home, connecting with others via zoom, was a perfect introduction. Now I love dancing in a physical space with others, showing up and being seen in movement continues to be a powerful experience for which I am so deeply grateful.
>
> Sarah Mills

> Through dance I interact with all aspects of myself that I am aware of, allowing me to inhabit my body more fully, feet connect with Mother Earth, while I connect on other levels, too.

Sometimes I dance with my inner shadow, feel its darker texture and I negotiate with myself, to transform it through movement. Or I let myself soar with my inner light. I feel my energy-body expand like a layer of "dense air" that surrounds me, and sometimes I invite others to enter "my" space. Like dancing in another realm of time and space, beyond the physical realm, before I return home, into my physical body.

Dominique Le Vin

> Dance your cares away. And let the music play!

Dance opens my heart. It refreshes mind, body and soul, while staying in the moment, so that all else washes away. It always improves my mood and helps to release stuck emotions.

Dance awakens every cell, every fibre of your being, whilst giving you heightened energy and vitality, even long after you have been dancing. When I dance, I can express myself. Anyone can do it. No matter what age/size/shape. I didn't start dancing at Flomotion until I was in my mid-70s.

How great to come together, bond and co-create our experience on the dancefloor. It's also wonderful to be invited to dance solo.

Dance is the rhythm of life! It heightens your self-esteem and by doing so it you know that anything is possible.

Sue

> I am originally from Iran. For a long time I had been looking for a more 'wholesome' dance experience. I absolutely love dancing. I am not a drug user and found

that in this country partying and dance come along with lots of noise, drugs and a hectic environment. The rave scene is emotionally and physically unsafe and can leave me regretful about the experience at the end.

I have travelled a lot in the Mediterranean. The dance opportunities there are a lot less druggy, and you can dance in open spaces. I was craving this. After lockdown I felt that I needed to go back to dance. I searched for dance classes but wanted something freer.

When I came to Flomotion, the experience was amazing. It was safe, the music was great, and the atmosphere calm and friendly. It didn't matter to me that I was the youngest person there; I could fit in well because people were friendly; it is a very safe environment. I am normally very analytical and self-conscious when I move, but when I am at Flomotion I can drop that. I am encouraged to be less self-conscious which is a relief.

I was looking for something therapeutic and more embodied. It is also a community experience. Flomotion is relatable and inviting for everyone. The pizza sessions afterwards are so cool as well; it feels good to hang out together after dancing.

The goal of Flomotion is about dancing, awareness and being allowed to feel what you want; it's not about how you look. Sometimes it brings up challenging feelings, but that's good. I am often able to let go of feelings after the meditation part of the session. I am proud that I can be closer my feelings; that's important to me.

Yasamin

FIVE

Conscious Dance practices today

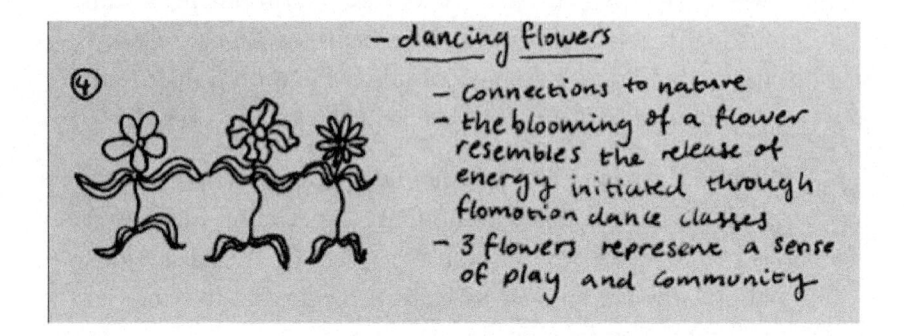

> — dancing flowers
> — connections to nature
> — the blooming of a flower resembles the release of energy initiated through flomotion dance classes
> — 3 flowers represent a sense of play and community

Who's dancing?

It's hard to know how many people are practising conscious dance around the world, but what is clear is that is growing fast. It is estimated that there are around 100 different types of conscious dance practice today, with more on the way. They range in their orientation: some more ecstatic, others more mindful or shamanistic.

The 5Rhythms website invites people to join the '100,000-plus feet dancing every year all around the world'; Open Floor has 'changed lives' in over 30 countries (and counting); and there are very many other conscious dance practices: Movement Medicine, Soul Motion, Chakra Dance, Azul, Biodanza, Zero One, Freedom Dance, Dancing Freedom and more. The Conscious Dance Conference held in 2019 was attended by 14,000 people from 94 countries.

A recent article in London's Evening Standard newspaper by Emma Thornton says that Ecstatic Dance 'is now sweeping the globe'. xxi The pandemic and the growth of social media has created new platforms and audience for Ecstatic dance to proliferate, and for new leaders to emerge. In the city where I live, London, I could participate in some sort of conscious dance every day of the week, often with choices about which session to attend.

What's the difference? The Common elements of Conscious Dance Practices

People sometimes ask how conscious dance is different from just having a dance with your mates at a party. If you are thinking about accepting my invitation to start dancing again, and want to join a conscious dance session, here are ten things you should expect:

i. Intention and Leadership

Conscious dance is not a party it's a practice, more like a workshop or yoga class in intention. It is entirely non-verbal, other than if the teacher has included an exercise to be shared verbally (eg in a particular part of the class). Its intention is towards healing and wellbeing. The Process: conscious dance has a shape:- a beginning, middle and end. There are times in a session to rest and digest, to integrate the dance/movement that has happened. Social events and parties are not usually curated in this way.

There is a facilitator or teacher, ideally one with some training to create an atmosphere of safety in which people can release and surrender to the process. The teacher will often be working with a system or plan for the session.

ii. Timing and the Movement Cycle

A conscious dance tends not be associated with nightlife activity and therefore often takes place at other times in the day. One of the most successful ecstatic dance sessions currently in London at the Hackney Baths takes place on a Sunday morning.

Dancing is decoupled from the world of discos, celebratory events, raves and becomes more aligned with the timetables of yoga, meditation and classes of other movement styles. None of these would necessarily happen at night. A conscious dance begins and ends at a particular time, again like a yoga or tai chi class. This is a boundaried container in which processes can happen. Often admission is not possible once the session is underway to avoid disrupting the atmosphere.

Dance movement practices often follow a pattern or movement cycle. This is a blueprint for the kind of music played (eg upbeat, peaceful etc) and the kind of atmosphere or feeling it is intended to evoke. In 5Rhythms dance, the cycle is expressed as a 'Wave' of 5 different rhythms of music. Open Floor dance uses a movement cycle loosely based on the Gestalt experience/awareness model: Open attention, Enter, Explore and Settle. Ecstatic Awakening Dance has a Warm up, Awakening life force, Let go, Stillness and Grounding.

iii. No steps, few lyrics.

Most dance practices use music that is predominantly instrumental, partly so that people can hear the facilitator's instructions more easily over the music and perhaps to encourage a more **embodied rather than cognitive response** to the sounds.

Instrumental music creates more opportunity for what is described as movement vocabulary (or movement range). When we dance to music with lyrics, especially ones we know well, we often fall into habitual patterns of movement. The practices offer the opportunity to try out different ways of moving and experiencing ourselves on the dancefloor. This can be a portal to finding different ways of 'being' in life.

There are no steps to learn: conscious dance is entirely about improvised or unchoreographed movement. It is less about mastering a technique and much more about being in the flow. It is nothing to do with performance.

iv. Non verbal

Conscious dance practices are explicit about leaving phones and chat at the door. This is often what is desired in other social dance settings but is not made so explicit and can result in long and loud conversations happening whilst others are trying to get deep into their groove.

There is a clear intention: to move with awareness, to breathe, to enter more deeply into the experience of the moving body. Some conscious dance practices talk about switching off the 'thinking' or 'monkey' mind, the incessant commentary and reactive thinking that we employ in life off the dancefloor.

Our normal conversational patterns of relating are paused. The invitation is to find ways to relate that are non-verbal. This is rich, illuminating and often unchartered experience for many.

v. No Booze/Drugs

You will not find a bar selling alcohol at a conscious dance practice. Neither will there be any drugs. An ecstatic dance may offer a Cacau ceremony, where you are offered a cocoa-like drink with a very mild psychoactive effect.

Indeed one of the reasons why ecstatic dance has grown exponentially is that many people are burnt out from the drugs and alcohol of the rave scene but want to feel the joy and bonding of the dancefloor. After a conscious dance session, you will feel released and revived. No need for substances.

vi. A Community: not a performance, and no spectators

As we have seen, moving with people forms bonds between them. Perhaps the most important aspect of these practices is that people feel closer to each other, that they feel connected to themselves and that they belong to the group. The value of this, in our increasingly digitised, remote and fragmented world, is inestimable.

There is no performative aspect of conscious dance practices. In our culture, people tend to associate dancing either with celebrations (weddings, Christmas/birthday parties) or with a performance (ballet/contemporary etc). Conscious dance is 'inside out' practice where what matters isn't dancing to an external formular or standard. Rather it is about using your awareness of breath and body in order to become more and more present, much like meditation.

There is no hierarchy or expert. It's not about doing anything for others. Nor is it about perfecting a technique. Being in community is a big part of all conscious dance practices.

vii. Dressing Up, Dressing Down

More often than not in Western culture, dancing is for special occasions, and we want to look our best by wearing smart clothes, makeup, jewellery, shoes etc. Whilst conscious dance practices are not prescriptive about what to wear, most will suggest comfortable clothes to move in. One core theme is that the dance is done, where possible, in bare feet. This is to feel a connection to the earth and the ground.

The inside/outside orientation of conscious dance also inclines people to be less concerned with what they *look* like in favour of what they *feel* like.

viii. In the body

There is a tendency in Western culture to be shy and self-conscious around dance. Most people are more comfortable sharing their thoughts than sharing their body movements with others. When people first come to sessions it can seem strange seeing people move with such a lack of inhibition.

Conscious dance, as the name implies, is about being conscious, moving and breathing with awareness. At parties, the onus is on 'getting out of it'; in conscious dance it's about 'getting into it' – being present and aware of how we can express feelings, thoughts and experience. Sometimes our bodies might just need to be lying still or moving gently on the floor.

Having a movement cycle, as described above, means that everyone is invited into a process from the beginning of a session. And because the vast majority of people will be following the invitation, it is easier to join in rather than not. The lack of alcohol and drugs to 'oil the wheels' to aid inhibition is perhaps paradoxically another encouragement; no one is waiting to come up or get high.

ix. Inclusion and diversity

Conscious dance is about freedom and inclusion. Everyone is welcomed to the space, to be themselves and find expression through the moving body, regardless of age, race, sexual orientation. There is an emphasis on turning up exactly as you are regardless of how you are feeling in mind or body.

Because there are no prescribed routines and the experience is non-verbal, there is freedom outside of the usual constraints of social interaction. Despite this, dancefloors are often not massively diverse and are predominantly populated by white, middle class, able bodied people. Open Floor, amongst others, is deeply committed to bringing more diversity to the dance space.

x. Don't forget the resistance!

As we have seen, there are historic reasons, religious and political, why dancing has been trained out of us in the Western world. Fear of humiliation and looking stupid also keeps people off dancefloors, especially when those dancefloors are the stone cold sober ones of conscious dance. Most of us have had the experience at social gatherings and parties when we feel a bit shy and self-conscious. There's someone who is keen to get the party started pulling and cajoling others onto the dancefloor. It can feel a bit forced. Many people will simply say 'I can't dance', which means they are too self-conscious to try.

Even teachers of conscious dance and those who become deeply committed to regular movement practice, often report their first (and subsequent) attendance at sessions as far from being a magnetic pull to the dance space. It can be threatening to be asked not to talk and only to relate through our moving bodies. Newcomers can find the lack of inhibition of seasoned dancers 'weird' and 'strange'; they can feel alienated and an outsider in the experience.

Once the culture shock of being and moving freely with others fades and there is an acclimatisation to non-conversational ways of relating, people sense other needs that *are* being met in the space: a feeling of connection, freedom and joy, a sense of belonging and being seen, being acknowledged exactly as you are, inclusion in community.

> My experience of conscious dance in its various iterations has been that it meets many needs: physical, emotional, psychological and spiritual. The dance leads me through the layers.
>
> Over time it has become much less about 'performance' and much more about expression. My body knows what it wants and needs and all I have to do is to 'get out of its way'. The space, the leader, the music and the other

dancers all play an integral role in determining what happens on a given day. Very often it feels like a deeply integrating experience happening out of conscious awareness.

Pernille Finegan

Conscious Dance Practices today.

Now that we know some of the common elements in conscious dance practices, let's look at some of the distinctive dimensions and differences between them. (By the way, many dancers participate in several conscious dance styles!). So, what are the conscious dance practices to get to know?

5Rhythms

5Rhythms was the first Ecstatic Dance 'practice'. Gabrielle Roth, founder of 5R, started developing her work in the 1960s. There hadn't been anything quite like it before. She wrote:

> *'I want to take you to a place of pure magic, where everything goes and nothing stops, like a twenty-four-hour roadside café with the best jukebox you can imagine…It's a place of pure light that holds the dark within it. It's a place of pure rhythm that holds the stillpoint. It's a place within you.'* G Roth

The 5R are described as a 'way of being'. They follow a 'wave' or pattern of music, suggestive of 5 moods or rhythms: flowing, staccato, chaos, lyrical and stillness. A facilitator will not only be playing music but will also be talking to the dancers; inviting more breath, bringing awareness to thoughts, feelings, sensations in the body, inviting release and let go.

The first half an hour of a 5R session is allowing people to warm up, stretch, begin to connect with breath and body. The music will probably be relaxing and easy. There may be some time where the teacher will name different body parts (eg, feet, legs, hips etc) to help people drop attention into their body.

The music will then reflect the different moods of the 5 Rhythms, with the teacher guiding. The teacher may play 2 or 3 tracks for each of the rhythms, and then might begin at 'flowing' for another wave. Sometimes there will be a suggestion to take a partner or join a few people dancing. Sometimes everyone will be in a big circle and invited to come and dance in the middle. xxii

Ecstatic Dance

Ecstatic Dance as we know it today only began to emerge in the 1990s. There was no one leader as Gabriel Roth is to 5R. The people who developed Ecstatic Dance knew and had practised 5R but didn't necessarily want to be part of that world and could see other ways to take the work forward drawing on shamanistic practices, altered states, ritualistic ceremonies, gong baths and more.

Having been on the scene when Ecstasy and Raving began to emerge in the 1980s, it seems that Ecstatic Dance has evolved partly as a consequence of these, unlike 5R, whose lineage is not directly related.

There was a lot of burn out, and probably still is, from persistent drug use and up-all-night raving. Having been turned on to the joy and liberation of the freedom to dance, people wanted to find less toxic and more sustainable ways to enjoy these things. Ecstatic Dance has produced offers such as 'Sober Raving' and 'Conscious Clubbing'.

Ecstatic Dance tends to follow a rave or nightclub pattern by having a DJ rather than a teacher. In a 2 hour session, there might be a cacao (cocoa-like drink with mild psychoactive properties) ceremony. The dance might follow a loose movement cycle: warm up, shaking (to release stress), free dance, rest and meditation. Dancers can be invited to do the whole or part of the session with eyes shut. The music might echo more of the rave experience: house, techno, trance, drum & bass, tribal. There will also be slower music for periods of rest and integration.

Organisers of Ecstatic Dance UK, describe the dance as:

'a meditation, a practice, a party, a workout and therapy. All of the above'. They say that in response to the proliferation in digital technologies and artificial intelligence there is a growing 'instinctive calling to something that is humanising. Something that brings us back down to earth and into our bodies.' xxiii

Open Floor

I have been lucky enough to do a 4 year teacher training with Open Floor, a practice that evolved after Gabrielle Roth died in 2012, from a number of practitioners who had worked with her over many years. Here is what they say about the practice:

'Open Floor is a resource based movement practice. We explore new ways of moving and responding to what is happening with intention and purpose. We learn to understand our habits and patterns for deeper insight and self-awareness. The more we embody different responses in our movements, the more resources we can call on to move through life with flexibility, resilience, and ease.' xxiv

The themes that Open Floor articulates and explores are found in all embodied practices. They are: release, ground, centre, pause, dissolve, vector, spatial awareness, expand and contract, towards and away, activate and settle.

An Open Floor movement session is about 2 hours long. It begins with bringing attention to breath and to how you find yourself: physically, emotionally, mentally and spiritually. Attention will then be drawn to a specific body part. The facilitator will suggest ways to move more deeply into the felt sense of this part of the body, solo or with a partner. Awareness shifts to the whole body, and there will be movement exploration of a theme such as Release or Spatial Awareness. The group will then have time to dance without guidance, and the session finishes with settling a chance to slow down and integrate all that has happened in the session. Open Floor is a powerful and transformative practice.

Movement Medicine™

Movement Medicine grew out of 5Rhythms. It was devised in the 1990s by Susannah and Ya'Acov Darling Khan who had both taught and danced with Gabriel Roth. They also draw on the wisdom of neuroscience, shamanistic, artistic and therapeutic practices. They work with simple practices to access the stories we hold in the body through breath and body awareness.

The model uses the 'The Movement Medicine Mandala' map of resources with '21 stations' representing 'the tree of life' which contains the 4 elements, 5 dimensions of awareness, 9 gateways (journeys of: empowerment, responsibility manifesting the dream), and in the centre the phoenix representing the Great Mystery, alongside the polarities of Yin and Yang.

A class begins with free movement and no guidance, giving people a chance to arrive and drop into breath and body awareness. There is than an opening sharing circle, and the facilitator will explain the theme of the class.

Thereafter there is movement and dancing to a carefully selected soundscape inviting a deeper awareness into the felt sense of self and body. The goal is to feel released and replenished.

The session ends with a closing circle where people share their experience. xxv

Biodanza

Biodanza, literally meaning the Dance of Life, is a dance practice and system to connect with joy. It is holistic in its approach, and is interested in human connection, education and social change. It improves confidence, joy of life and human connection. The music is uplifting and from around the world.

Like 5Rhythms dance, Biodanza was created in the 1960s against the backdrop of the destruction of WW2, the holocaust, the atomic bomb and large scale destruction of human populations. There was also a drive towards love and human connection with nature, and a belief that positive life changes motivate people to live to their greatest human potential.

The founder of Biodanza was Rolando Toro Araneda, A Chilian Psychologist. Here's what he said about the practice:

> *"Biodanza...addresses the totality of the human being. It doesn't separate people into fragments. Biodanza has many therapeutic effects, but these are not the goal."*

> *"The word Biodanza has two parts, bios (life) and danza (meaningful movement). So Biodanza is the possibility of dancing our own lives, of bringing music, rhythm, harmony and emotion into our communities and personal lives. Biodanza is different from conventional dance because it's a guided discipline that stimulates specific aspects of human potential, such as creativity, affection, vitality, and so forth, through different sets of movement to music exercises."*

Biodanza is currently practised in 54 countries around the world, including many European countries, the USA, Russia, India, Australia and Brazil. xxvi

Flomotion

Flomotion is my own particular conscious dance offer. It takes place every 2 weeks in person, currently meeting at in a church hall in Archway, North London. There are also online dance sessions. The music reflects my lifetime interest in Jazz, reggae, house, funk, soul, Latin and Global Grooves. The structure is drawn from a number of conscious dance practices including Ecstatic Dance and Open Floor..

At the beginning of the session we form a circle, and everyone says their name. Then the music goes on and the following 2 hours are about movement not words. The first couple of tracks are relaxed music, inviting people to arrive in the session in any way that's comfortable for them. Stretching, yawning etc. We then move into a full body warm up as I describe different body parts. There is lots of reference to breath and bringing awareness into the body.

'The Shake' is next, taken from Ecstatic Awakening Dance, it's sometimes called trauma release. It's a movement I demonstrate (knees bobbing up and down, rest of the body soft) that's designed to release stress and tension that we hold in our bodies. We often do this to a funk track. After the Shake, I ask people to turn to a pair of feet next to theirs. I encourage them to move to the music welcoming these feet with their own. I then move people to a different pair of feet and repeat the process. This repeats so that ideally everyone encounters everyone else in the space. It often evokes laughter and fun.

There are then a few tracks (Latin, Ska, Disco, House etc) in which people get to dance in their own way. I reassure them that there are no right or wrong moves; just welcoming their own movement. Attention to breath, moving around the space where possible, and if wanted, echoing and offering parts of their dance to and with others.

A couple of slow, peaceful tracks come on as I offer some space for relaxation or gentle movement. Often people lie on the floor at this point to revive their energy. As people are still resting, I talk them through the next part of the Flomotion experience where we practice the 'Inner Dance'. Many people say this is their favourite part of the session. People are invited to close their eyes and dance from this place 'like nobody's watching', because they're not. People do this part of the dance both on the floor, standing and in between.

I often choose music here that evokes feeling or speaks to our vulnerability. It's a safer space to access this in the privacy of our inner worlds and informs movement in many ways. Afterwards, I invite people to open their eyes and to bring their movement back to the shared dance space. We then begin another cycle of free dance. If the group looks lost, I might offer more guidance through the microphone. Other times, the group energy is enough.

For the penultimate track, I stop the music and invite half of the group to go to one wall, and the other half to the opposite wall. I explain that the first group will move across the room with the others cheering and encouraging. We then swap. The music is deep and funky. The two groups then finally meet in the middle, and we dance together.

The final track comes on, usually something rousing, about love or otherwise uplifting. This is usually a time of joyous connection. Finally, we settle again onto chairs and the floor, the music is relaxing, and I do a gentle guided meditation. We gather in a circle at the end to share a few words about our experience. xxvii

> I love the shape of flomotion. The path, sequence or journey each session takes us through. We normally arrive full of external influence and the first part of the sequence helps you land, get grounded and warm up. The shake loosens us takes us out of ourselves and further grounds we then dance which is fantastic.
>
> Then we slow down with a relaxation and taken through the inner dance to our internal world. This is a place of self discovery. We then dance and share and interact and

flow with each other which is wonderful. It all culminated in a fantastic guided meditation that settles the journey and gives it personal meaning.

Francisco Cruzat

> Flomotion's structure is like nothing else. It holds my hand and is by my side the whole time. Starting off with gentle and ambient sounds, where I get a feel for the session. Then, the 'Shake' - a brilliant way to wake up the whole body.
>
> After that it's full swing with anything from Soul to Funk to Afro to Lounge to Irish Jigs. Interspersed with lovely introspective periods – a guided meditation, and 'inner dance' with eyes closed. Dancing with others, purely optional, and in groups, add to the mix. The whole session brings light and love into my being.

David Cohen

> Flomotion, to me, is a journey of discovery, and each session delivers something new – movement I never knew I had, emotions I never knew were there, and music that inspires joy and creativity. We're always warmly welcomed to the space, and each other, through gentle movements, then as the pace picks up, we shake off any stress, feeling lighter and uplifted as we travel through an eclectic playlist of genres from funk, soul, and latin, to some banging club classics. In fact, at times, when the fun and playful energy is buzzing, I feel like a teenager again out clubbing in London!
>
> Relaxation and meditation punctuate the sessions, providing an opportunity for rest and reflection on the sensations that have arisen through the dance, and the

inner dance section connects us to ourselves in a safe and non-judgemental way. It's a transformative experience every time, and I always leave feeling calm, relaxed, peaceful, and centred, despite how exhausted and stressed I may have felt when I arrived!

Lisa Taylor

But wait, there's more...

Other conscious dance practice are Soul Motion, FreedomDance, Azul Conscious Movement, ZeroOne. And there are many more. xxviii-xxxi

There are two professional organisations in the conscious movement world. One is The International Conscious Dance Movement Teacher's Association (ICMTA)xxxii which uphold professional and ethical standards in the profession. It supports ongoing education and a collective and collaborative approach.

The other is The Dance First Association xxxiii which provides resources, promotion and support to the global community of movement teachers and practices. They produce Conscious Dancer Magazine, founded in 2007, reaching 100,000 people in hundreds of international locations.

The One Dance Tribe offers a global conscious dance movement community of senior teachers and 'world class healers'. xxxiv

In this chapter we have taken the wide view, side steps, to look at the field of conscious movement practice. We have seen that there are some themes that run through most of these practices which include the opportunity for community, a no drugs/no booze space, non-verbal participation, non- performance, drawing awareness to body and breath, inclusion of all experience and all people.

So far we have seen the pivotal nature of dance in the evolution of humanity, its powerful effects of pulling people together and great potential for healing, and how the conscious dance movement is taking this forward especially in creating places of connection and belonging.

> What is this thing that we do, this thing called dance? Moving the whole body or parts – arms, legs, head, shoulders, hands, fingers, feet – if we move them one way then we feel a certain way, move another way, and it's a different path, a different feeling. Taking a risk – what move are we going to make next? Tiny movements, thus leading to small changes...and it's these types of small changes that really make the difference in our wellbeing, in our dealing with life. Small steps, not giant strides. Try it, take a risk, move another way, and feel the difference.
>
> Edgar Jones

> My recent diagnosis of stage 4, metastatic breast cancer has been challenging in every way - physically, mentally and emotionally. It has brought into sharp relief what is important in life - spending quality time with those you love most and doing the things that you enjoy and make you feel valued, supported and loved. Dancing has always been one of my passions - It helps me to feel present, to focus on the now and often temporarily suspends intrusive thoughts.
>
> As well as the physical exercise it can help to lift my mood and I feel happy and joyful connecting with others. The Flomotion sessions provide an opportunity to meet and connect with others who love dancing. It is a space to dance both on my own, delving into my inner world and also to come together in pairs or with the whole group - mirroring each others' movements is

uplifting and fun - it creates a very special connection between the participants.

Flomotion provides a space where I can let go and be myself and dance without judgement. It always makes me happy and I leave feeling more positive and connected both with my fellow dancers and the wider community. It is so beneficial and special on so many levels - I feel safe and nurtured, which is so important during my current sometimes stressful and challenging circumstances.

Angela Cross

I hope this book has inspired you to get dancing. It's your birth right, and a lifetime of culturally imposed inhibition, preoccupation with the perceived judgement of others, and a tendency to hold back, in my view is a life not well lived.

Perhaps the book has filled in some gaps about dance and what it can offer. You might now know that there are opportunities to engage in regular dance without having to learn steps, be in a nightclub or at a party. It may have put words to your own intuitive sense that when you dance good things are happening: mind, body and soul. The voices of the dancers in the book may pick up some threads of your own experience and I hope will inspire you to get involved with some conscious dance yourself. You might be hungry for connection and community and can see that dancing together is an easy and fulfilling way in. You might just want to have more fun in your life.

One thing is for sure, if more of us danced there would be more opportunities to get together and connect through our moving bodies, with all the benefits: social, emotional, physical, intellectual. We'd also get more chance to play, something woefully lacking in responsible adult hood. There are no downsides to dance (although injury prevention is important and it's something most conscious dance practices give attention to).

Diary of a Conscious Dance Teacher, Saturday

We've arrived! The dance is this evening. I charge up my beloved Rode wireless microphone. Select a meditation. I haven't touched the playlist for a few days. It needs to rest, ferment. There is always the risk of listener fatigue, killing the joy of the underlying pattern and arc of experience. I have needed some space from it to listen anew.

I put my EarPods in and head for the park. A final run though of the playlist. It's okay, actually it's quite good. I picture the dancing bodies; they seem to like it. I like it. The afternoon comes round and I'm packing the car with large speakers, stands and two big rucksacks filled with lights, leads, a lamp, microphone, computer and more. We head for the church hall in Archway.

It's now 30 minutes until the doors open. My crew are busy doing final touches to the room: getting water, checking the toilets, taping down the lighting where they've cleverly demarked the dancefloor, turning this basic, utilitarian 1930s space into a sparkly, exciting groove space. There's a big red heart on the floor made from the rope lighting. The speakers and cables have gone up, a fold-up table covered with black sheet serves as the DJ desk: laptop, mixer, mic transmitter, light, playlist, notes. I am doing a soundcheck with the mic. Screeching sounds bring yelps from the crew when I get too near the speakers. Someone is spraying the room cleanser carefully made by my friend, Emily, to clear the atmosphere and ready us to create our own energy. The small disco ball has gone up in the corner.

I read the room, choosing some mellow music to test the

sound. Sometimes sound is only coming from one speaker, I have to check all the cables and connections, stress rising when there isn't an obvious fault. Breathe, breathe, breathe.

I remember something from my Open Floor training. It's about gratitude for all the teachers who have influenced me, who have helped me take steps to this dancefloor; all the musicians who make the music that I have the privilege to select; all my family and friends who have supported and encouraged me along the way. I channel the energy of one dance teacher who has really touched and inspired me. Feel her in my bones, feel her encouraging gaze on me. I move and breathe her. It's grounding, reassuring.

The buzzer goes and moments later the first person arrives. Big smiles, hugs, warmth, belonging. More bodies fill the room. People get settled, changing clothes, taking off shoes, going to the toilet, pouring water. We're ready to dance once again!

As I write the last part of this book, I can't sign off without speaking directly to the felt sense of your moving body.

Here's the steer:

Take a few deep, slow breaths, down into your stomach.

Find a piece of music (probably on your phone/computer/tablet) that makes you feel upbeat, energised, happy.

As you listen, let your shoulders sway, nod your head, make patterns with your hands, sway your hips, let your feet take you on a walk around your space. Give yourself time. As you move, pay attention to your breath, allow it to deepen. Let yourself be moved by the music.

Notice any feelings that you become aware of as you move (happy/sad/anything). They're just feelings, they live in our bodies and when we move, they come to the surface. You might even want to welcome them, certainly find ways to move them.

Above all follow in the steps of your ancestors: Move, Be Free…

Dance For Life.

Acknowledgments

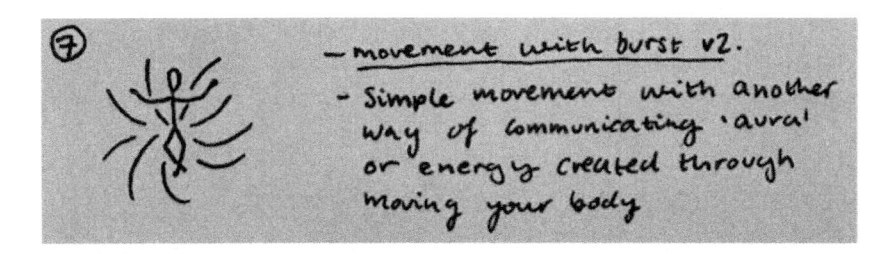

> — movement with burst v2.
> - Simple movement with another way of communicating 'aural' or energy created through moving your body

I like to read the acknowledgements in books. They give a context to the writing and tell me more about who matters to the author, and other people whose ideas and investment lie in the background of the words I have been reading.

In this book, the territory is mapped by the dancing steps of many who have joined me on the dancefloor over the years, quite a few of whom are quoted in this book (big thank you). I am immensely grateful to you all. I could not have been on this journey without you.

Deep gratitude goes out to some diligent readers and contributors: my husband, who has had to put up with my self-doubt (frequent), grumpiness (sometimes) and loss of hope (occasionally). Thank you, G. This book would never have come together without your support and encouragement.

Pat Mary – thank you for your kind words of encouragement. Many years ago you told me I could write; you told me I had a voice; you believed in my ability. You also kindly proof read, contributed and gave feedback for this book.

David Cohen – you have been a great supporter of Flomotion over a long period of time for which I am very grateful. Thank you for proof-reading this book and offering ideas and edits. Also for the lively guest blogs you have contributed to the Flomotion website.

Jim Kinloch – for your ongoing help with my marketing, encouraging me to write blogs and for giving me the idea to write a book.

Finola Kinloch- for your beautiful and original artwork that line the pages of this book.

My friends who have supported and encouraged me along the way – thank you.

The many teachers who I have been lucky enough to learn from in the Open Floor, 5Rhythms and Ecstatic Dance worlds.

My gratitude to my beloved parents who let me take the path that I wanted to follow, always.

Gratitude to our children for putting up with my dancing, and a mum who's a bit 'weird and out there' at times.

Bibliography

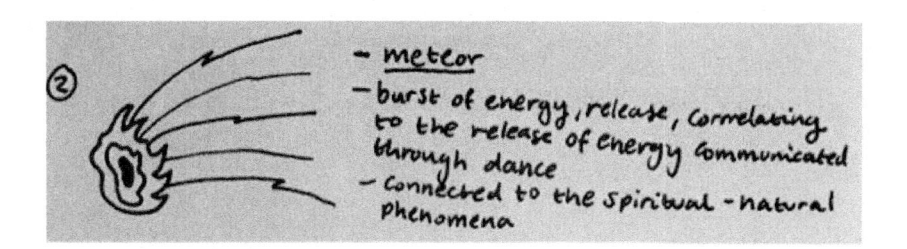

— meteor
— burst of energy, release, correlating to the release of energy communicated through dance
— Connected to the spiritual - natural phenomena

Christensen, Julia F and Chang, Dong-Seon *Dancing is the Best Medicine* (Greystone Books 2021)

Payne, Helen (Ed), *Dance Movement Therapy* (Routledge 2006)

Ehrenreich, Barbara, *Dancing in the Streets: A History of Collective Joy* (Granta 2007)

Warren, Emma, *Dance Your Way Home* (Faber 2023)

Amoda, *Moving Into Ecstasy: An Urban Mystic's Guide to Movement, Medicine and Meditation* (Thorsons 2001)

McNeill, William H, *Keeping Together in Time: Dance and Drill in Human History* (Harvard University Press 1995)

Ferrucci, Piero, *Inevitable Grace: Breakthroughs in the lives of great men and women: guides to your self-realization* (Tarcher Penguin 1990)

Roth, Gabrielle, *Sweat Your Prayers, Movement as Spiritual Practice* (Newleaf 1991)

Roth, Gabrielle, *Maps to Ecstasy: teachings of an urban shaman* (Mandala 1990)

Payne, Helen, *Dance Movement Therapy: theory, research and practice* (Routledge 2008)

Gendlin, Eugene T, *Focusing How to gain direct access to your body's knowledge* (Rider 2003)

Dana, Deb, *Polyvagal Exercises for Safety and Connection* (Norton 2020)

Eisenstein, Charles, *The More Beautiful World Our Hearts Know is Possible* (North Atlantic Books 2013)

Barley, Adam, *Pathways Home* (Adambarley.com 2022)

Dychtwald, Ken, *Bodymind* (Tarcher Putnam 1986)

Van der Kolk, Bessel, *The Body Keeps The Score* (Penguin 2015)

Haidt, Jonathan, *The Righteous Mind* (Penguin 2012)

Mindell, Arnold, ProcessMind (Quest Books 2010)

Mindell, Arnold, *Quantum Mind and Healing* (Hampton Roads 2004)

Mindell, Arnold, *The Shaman's Body* (Harper Collins 1993)

Hanna, Judith Lynne, *Dancing for Health, conquering and preventing stress* (AltaMira Press 2006)

Lovatt, Dr Peter, *The Dance Cure* (Short Books 2020)

Bibliography

Walker, Alice, *Hard Times Require Furious Dancing* (New World Library 2010)

Rosenberg, Stanley, *Acccessing The Healing Power of the Vagus Nerve* (North Atlantic Books 2017)

Karkou, Vicky; Oliver, Sue; Lycouris, Sophia (Eds), The Oxford Handbook of Dance and Wellbeing (Oxford University Press 2017)

Siegel, Daniel, *Mindsight* (One World 2011)

Cozolino, Louis, The Neuroscience of Human Relationships (WW Norton & Company 2013)

Rogers, Susan and Ogas, Oggi, This Is What It Sounds Like (Penguin 2023)

End Notes

1. https://www.theguardian.com/theguardian/2007/may/26/weekend7.weekend5
2. https://www.independent.co.uk/arts-entertainment/all-funned-out-you-need-therapy-1312445.html
3. https://www.processwork.org/
4. https://thereader.mitpress.mit.edu/it-turns-out-we-were-born-to-groove/
5. https://dancefacts.net
6. https://wecoregulate.com/
7. https://www.iti-worldwide.org/
8. https://iadms.org/
9. https://www.bbc.co.uk/programmes/articles/1Hpr6R1f4M7f8Qc6fPGH2hg/why-dancing-is-the-best-way-to-enhance-your-brain-and-fitness
10. https://independentdance.co.uk/wp-content/uploads/2022/08/Mind-As-In-Motion-Gill-Clarke-2007.pdf
11. https://www.nytimes.com/2023/12/26/arts/dance/dance-in-2023-the-cool-genre.html?unlocked_article_code=1.MU0.DHzH.Nk6KQQbcFwhx&smid=nytcore-ios-share&referringSource=articleShare
12. https://www.trinitylaban.ac.uk/dance-health-and-wellbeing-findings-published/
13. https://www.nationalgeographic.com/travel/article/how-dance-connects-people-during-coronavirus
14. https://www.england.nhs.uk/personalisedcare/social-prescribing/#:~:text=What%20is%20social%20prescribing%3F,affect%20their%20health%20and%20wellbeing
15. https://www.theguardian.com/commentisfree/2022/dec/22/im-an-older-man-and-i-love-to-dance-whats-wrong-with-that
16. https://www.theguardian.com/music/2024/feb/11/daytime-clubbing-rave-generation-day-fever-club-london-outernet
17. https://admp.org.uk/
18. https://scottishballet.co.uk/move-with-us/dance-classes/time-to-dance/
19. https://www.dancenetworkassociation.org.uk/projects/dancing-with-dementia
20. https://www.uclahealth.org/news/free-moving-dance-has-healing-benefits-for-people-with-mental-health-concerns
21. https://fallenangelsdt.org/
22. https://www.standard.co.uk/lifestyle/ecstatic-dance-london-meaning-purpose-mindful-movement-b1067087.html
23. https://www.5rhythms.com/
24. https://ecstaticdance.org/dance/ecstatic-dance-uk/
25. https://openfloor.org/

End Notes

26. https://www.schoolofmovementmedicine.com/
27. https://www.biodanza.org/en/dance-of-life/
28. https://www.flomotion.dance/
29. https://soulmotioninternational.com/
30. https://freedom-dance.com/
31. https://pathofazul.com/
32. https://adambarley.com/zeroone/
33. https://www.icmta.com/
34. https://dancefirst.com/
35. https://onedancetribe.com/

Printed in Great Britain
by Amazon